HUMANIZING

B2B

The new truth in marketing that will transform your brand and your sales

T0145772

PAUL CASH AND JAMES TREZONA

First published in Great Britain by Practical Inspiration Publishing, 2021

© Paul Cash and James Trezona, 2021

The moral rights of the authors have been asserted.

ISBN   9781788602518 (print)
       9781788602501 (epub)
       9781788602495 (mobi)

Practical Inspiration
Publishing

'Paul Cash is the Jamie Oliver of B2B Marketing. His ideas, passion and enthusiasm are infectious. There is something tasty in this book for everyone. Go ahead and feed your soul.'

Joel Harrison, Co founder and Editor-in-chief at B2B Marketing

'Don't read this book! It will make you a better B2B marketer. Which makes it infinitely harder for the rest of us.'

Darryl Bowman, CMO at Receipt Bank

'This book is an indispensable guide for standing out right now in a crowded B2B world. Cash shines the light on the inconvenient truth, that in our quest for short term gains, we've lost sight of how to create brands that capture hearts and minds over the long haul. A must read.'

Nick Ashmore, VP of Marketing at ResponseTap

'*Humanizing B2B* is a rallying cry and essential reading for ambitious B2B marketers eager to transform their careers. It is a refreshing, inspiring and passionate tour de force of why emotion and storytelling must be placed at the heart of a business's brand and sales proposition. This book will take you on a journey of discovery that wonderfully blends theory with practical insights and strategies that will make your business stand out from the crowd and drive commercial success.'

Luke Lang, Co-founder and CMO at Crowdcube

'I really like how this book looks at the topic from different angles, including 'chemistry', literally! Plenty of real-life stories and meaningful advice. Clear messages to marketing: remember, the customer is a person like you, not a lead, a contact or a persona. And to the CEO/CFO: Being human is profitable.'

Jan Gladziejewski, Senior Marketer

'I'll admit it, I LOVE B2B marketing, always have, always will. I think at times it's seen as the poor relation to B2C as a discipline because it's perceived as not as 'human' or exciting. This book will change that. It clearly lays out why there has never been a more exhilarating time to work in the B2B space – it's a game changer on how to embed emotion and a sense of purpose into a strategy that drives transformational growth. This book is packed with brilliant ideas, examples of great work and a new philosophy for B2B marketing that could be career-defining for the next generation of marketers.'

Kath Easthope, VP Global Marketing at Phrasee

'This is a book that breaks down the barriers of brand building in B2B. For brand and lead generation marketers this is a must read. It's bold, informative and makes a compelling case that brand is demand. Humanizing B2B is the only way to go.'

Mark Bogaerts, Director Brand & Sponsorship Europe/UK at Tata Consultancy Services

Contents

Foreword

B2B marketing has come a long way in a such a short space of time. Since I've been involved in this industry, which is now terrifyingly 17 years, it's gone from being a sideshow, performed by geeks and techies, and not just looked down upon but utterly dismissed by anyone involved in mainstream, i.e. consumer marketing. But today, the outsider has become the mainstream. B2B has indisputably arrived – it is recognised, respected, regarded and rewarded as never before. B2B marketers no longer feel like they are any kind of poor relation – what they do is vibrant and valid, and in so many ways much more interesting than what happens 'over there', in consumer land.

There are many reasons for this transformation, but it's in no small part due to the passion and determination of advocates and evangelists like Paul and James. I met Paul very soon after we founded B2B Marketing magazine, back in 2004, and James not long afterwards. They share a restless energy, a creative mindset, and a passion for innovation or challenging the status quo that makes them a great partnership.

viii | Humanizing B2B

From the word go, Paul was a massive supporter of ours, encouraging us on to bigger and better things and generating ideas for new products and services so fast we could barely write them down. Paul and James were two of the key individuals who really drove the transformation and recognition of B2B as an industry throughout the noughties and the teens, and who are responsible for its dramatic change in status and appreciation in 2021.

But they both recognise that, although B2B's transformation to date has been beyond most practitioners' hopes or expectations, there's much, much more that's required. No industry can ever stand still, or rest on its laurels – the pandemic has made that abundantly clear. But more than that, there's more that we can achieve as professionals, and as a profession, if we're prepared to go further, for the benefit of both our brands and ourselves. And that's why *Humanizing B2B* is extraordinarily timely.

Thankfully, so much of the corporate BS advertising of the recent past has been consigned to the dustbin of history (quite rightly), and things like account-based marketing and the explosion in customer insight technology has done much to promote the understanding of the role of the individual in B2B decision making (not to mention offering the means and ability to identify protagonists). And yet so often, B2B marketing remains generic, impersonal and ignorant of its intended audience or their needs, desires, interests, quirks and foibles. There is so much more that we can, should, and must do, to understand and appeal to the human being at the other end of our marketing campaign.

We know that decision-making units are complex and only becoming more so. We know that buyers are becoming ever more fickle and savvy, expecting to do the overwhelming bulk of their research before they make themselves known to sales. Indeed, the ability of sales to influence their decision making in many B2B scenarios is (arguably) becoming increasingly marginal. It's marketing that's doing the heavy lifting, and to do that, to really move and engage people in 2021 and beyond, it needs to engage on a human level.

For me at least, there is no question about this direction of travel for B2B marketing, or what brands and marketers need to do to respond. If, like me, you've bought in to this profound shift, and are looking for ways or means of turning convictions into action, this book will provide you with practical and deliverable strategies to make your B2B more human, more compelling and more effective to boot. If you're yet to be convinced, it will give you the inspiration and the confidence to make that leap. Even having got this far, you're accepting that B2B marketing can and should aspire to being better, and that we need to be restless and inquisitive to understand how to make that happen.

B2B marketing has come such a long way, and its progress fills me with great confidence and excitement about the future as an industry. The future of B2B marketing is bright, the future is human.

Joel Harrison
Editor-in-chief
B2B Marketing

The meteor is coming

This is a book about you, the hero of our story. You're the much-loved, often-misunderstood wearer of many B2B marketing hats. The technologist, the strategist, the customer champion, the data expert, the creative leader, the analyst, the storyteller. You're the hard-working, ambitious B2B marketer of the current age, whether you're a chief marketing officer (CMO) or one of the younger generation of digital marketers wanting to leap ahead and win.

However – and we hate to say it – there's something that you don't know. There's a giant meteor spinning towards you, and it's going to have a catastrophic effect on your profession. This meteor is the inevitable consequence of B2B marketing's failings. And what would those failings be? Well, if you're like the vast majority of B2B marketers, you've probably been creating and promoting your products in much the same way for as long as you can remember. In simplified terms, it goes something like this.

o   You make or develop a product or service.
o   You spend a lot of time crafting messaging and content, focusing on the features and benefits your customers want.

o You use performance channels and platforms like Google, email marketing and social media to engage people.

o You build a sales funnel to move your prospects from 'awareness' to 'action'.

o You expect double – or triple – digit growth as a result.

So far, so good. But when the sales reps start asking their prospects if they're actually going to buy this amazing thing, the answer is mystifying: 'I don't have the budget at the moment – come back next year and we might have a re-think then.' What? It's like a dagger to the heart – mortifying. So you run away and hide behind your marketing key performance indicators (KPIs), assuming the problem must lie with the sales team.

Does this sound familiar? And why? The problem is that there's a limit to what this kind of product-centric marketing model can deliver for B2B businesses. Although it's the norm, it won't make your company stand out because it's *what everyone else is doing*. So you'll never achieve more than average results with it. Yet we've never heard anyone in marketing confess that 'being average' is their dream – that it fills them with pride, or is the reason they go to work each day. We're willing to bet it's not what you aspire to, either.

Unfortunately, the issue doesn't end there, because there's another problem to deal with and it's one that reared its head time and again when we interviewed various senior marketing leaders to broaden our understanding for this book. It's that the way a CMO talks to their marketing team is completely different to the way they talk to their board. With their teams, the CMO is happy to discuss strategy, branding and long-term customer relationships. But the moment they step into the boardroom, they're confronted by a chief executive officer (CEO) and chief financial officer (CFO) who see 'brand' as a dirty word – as something that sucks money out of the business rather than generating value. They want their CMO to create a predictable revenue machine (in other words, the lead generation tools and tech stack that you're only too familiar with). But what if our CMO were to ask their board what they *really* want from marketing? If they did, they'd surely learn it would be to make the company number one in its category or to take it somewhere new – in other words, to achieve transformational growth. This contradiction is essentially what this book helps you to deal with.

It's even more important to address this issue now that we're at such a critical and delicate moment in the world economy. Marketing leaders have to adapt and evolve, inspire others and add new ways of thinking to their roles. They require strategies that have an exponential rather than an incremental effect on sales, and to deliver them they need new super-skills. (We say 'they', but of course that's 'you'. You're probably starting to see why we're calling you a hero now.)

At this stage, we'd like to say that we make no apologies for being up-front in the way we've written this book. It's partly so that we can jolt your thinking, and partly because we need to be clear about what problems B2B marketing faces. But please be sure of one thing: we're only doing it because we know that, deep down, you care about our industry as much as we do. As stated by Richard Robinson, general manager at LeadFamly, 'B2B needs to step up, raise its game and put itself on the front foot.' And we agree – it needs to be the engine of growth and transformation in every B2B company. Why? Because B2B isn't just about short-term performance marketing, but about value and revenue creation through branding as well. If we don't radically change it, it will become marginalized – left to handle 'communications' and little else. As our hero, you can't let that happen.

It was an old friend of mine, Joanne Gilhooley, who was at the time marketing director at Hewlett-Packard Enterprise (and is now global marketing leader at Microsoft), who first gave me the perfect analogy for why B2B marketing is so average. 'Paul', she said, 'Marketing is a bunch of levers that need to be pulled. I'm not a marketing director, I'm a lever-puller.' By 'levers' she meant content marketing, email campaigns, Google Adwords and all the other tools of lead generation so beloved of B2B marketing. I could see the sadness in her eyes as she said this, but Joanne is an optimistic and innovative person who was torn between pulling levers and wishing she could break free and do something transformational instead. Luckily, Joanne has found a new home at Microsoft, where she's now free to bring a sense of purpose into her marketing. But if you've ever felt like Joanne once did, this book is for you.

So where does the meteor come in? After all, you're still on the first couple of pages. You've just discovered that you're the unwitting hero in a book about the inevitable demise of a profession you care deeply about, due to a mysterious chunk of rock heading your way. And it's up to you to do something about it. As the hero, you must embark on a quest to destroy the meteor and save B2B Land from its fate. While you journey through foreign territory you'll face countless challenges and naysayers, you'll find yourself battling convention and you'll even start questioning your own beliefs. However, have no fear, because we're here to guide you all the way, and it starts with you learning a new language.

The three languages

When you enter a new land you must master its language, and the first one anyone learns when they enter the world of B2B is that of the product. What does the product or service do? What are its features? What makes it perform better than the competition? How does it fit into the rest of the company's portfolio? Then, if you're a marketer, you also graduate to learning the language of the customer. What are their needs and challenges? How can you empathize with their situation? What ways can you best communicate your solution to their problem?

So far, so good, but this is where B2B gets stuck. Can you see the disconnect between the two languages? One is based on facts, the other on insight and understanding. It's as if there's something not quite right – a barrier stopping you from making a fluent transition from one to the other. You understand the need to move closer to your customer so you can see where they're coming from, but if you look around you, you'll see that very few B2B companies are turning their customer insights into powerful communications. That's because there's a third language you need to learn, which is the one that helps you to make that transition. It's the language of emotion, and mastering this changes everything.

Contrary to what seems to be the accepted view, B2B buyers respond to the language of emotion and will happily pay more for your products and services if they're spoken to in that language. It's the language of feelings, influence and clarity, encouraging your customers to buy again and again because it makes them feel positive about you. It's also the language of storytelling. If you take yourself back to the old days of charismatic B2B sales people, this is what they had in spades, but now these people are a dying breed and you need to learn what they always knew (and deploy it at scale through your marketing communications).

In other words…

o The language of product shows that you know what you're selling.
o The language of the customer shows that you know who you're selling to.
o The language of emotion shows that you know how to sell.

It goes further, because when you use the language of emotion internally it allows you to build amazing teams and tackle impossible challenges. You can give your career an edge that will have a direct impact on your earning power, and also discover a sense of gratification and completeness you may never have felt before. It's so much more compelling than pulling levers. Think how exciting it would be to fall in love with your job again, and to have something to feel buzzed about when you go to work. With 48% of B2B customers saying they feel bored by the marketing they see now, you're not the only one who's in need of a radical change.[1]

---

[1] Guta, M. (2019). 'Warning: 48% of B2B Buyers Bored by Most Marketing They See Right Now', Small Business Trends, 6 March. https://smallbiztrends.com/2019/03/b2b-marketing-statistics.html

You can see how it works in what we call the 'golden triangle'.

The golden triangle

Features within the diagram:
- TRANSFORMATIONAL GROWTH
- KNOW HOW TO SELL (The art of storytelling)
- THE LANGUAGE OF EMOTION
- WE ARE HERE AS AN INDUSTRY
- KNOW WHO YOU'RE SELLING TO (What are their needs?)
- THE LANGUAGE OF CUSTOMER
- THE EVOLUTION OF B2B MARKETING
- CONSCIOUS NEED
- UNCONSCIOUS NEED
- THE LANGUAGE OF PRODUCT
- KNOW WHAT YOU'RE SELLING (Features and benefits)

The golden triangle
© Rooster Punk 2021

So what does speaking the language of emotion mean in reality? It's that business audiences want more from you than product features and benefits, or 'speeds and feeds'. They want to be entertained, educated and made to feel special. They crave recognition and approval. They want to understand your company's sense of purpose and values so they can gain a feeling for its people and culture. They'd love to know what you care about, and they demand (or they would if there was an option) to see you demonstrate all of these elements in an authentic and meaningful way. In short, they want to be treated as human beings and not as buying machines. In modern B2B marketing the role of brand isn't just to make your customers feel good about your company, your product or your service; it's to make them feel good about themselves for choosing it. Be honest – is this how you're treating them?

The more closely you align your product with emotion, the greater the impact on your company's growth, the steeper your career trajectory and the more inspirational a leader you'll become. Just like learning any language, it's not an instant fix, but it's a quest well worth venturing on when you know what you can achieve. Given that the end purpose of all B2B marketing is to move minds rather than to fulfil meaningless KPIs such as website visits and costs per click, you're far better off becoming an expert in people and their feelings than in a limited set of marketing techniques.

What's wrong now

In B2B we suffer from a delusion, and it's this: that buyers always act in a rational, logical and economic way. They don't, and they never have. What's more, in recent years the tectonic plates of B2B have shifted and its customers have evolved. They don't just want to buy *from* you any more, they want to buy *into* you. This isn't just our opinion; it's validated by a series of landmark research pieces which prove that B2B audiences buy on emotion and justify with fact, just like their B2C counterparts.

You may be asking yourself how B2B has become mired in the 'average' mindset for so long, speaking only the language of products and, if we're lucky, customers. We've spent many years trying to answer this question, and have come to the conclusion that there are three factors at play. The first is that there's a broken line of communication between marketing and the board. The second is that there's a dominant, product-led mindset that's difficult to break. And the third is that there's a lack of investment in and understanding of the impact of brand. In addition, another consideration might be that marketers don't know any different, which leads them to do what everyone around them does and ignore the fact that brands like Microsoft, Salesforce, Apple and Google have managed to dominate (and create) their categories because they rejected the average path. This final point is the reason we've written this book: we want you to know different so you can do different.

The good news is that the B2B sector is crammed with bright, ambitious and talented people just like you. It's full of founders who want to leave their mark on the world, engineers and scientists who are reinventing the way we live our lives and technologists and business owners who are changing the way we learn and work. We feel proud that these people choose to operate in the world of B2B, and it saddens us to know that their achievements are often thwarted because the marketing they create is stuck in a rut.

You're better than this, and you can make a difference. It simply entails shifting your focus from products to people, accepting that buyers and decision makers want empathy and engagement with their issues. It means turning your marketing attention from features to feelings, acknowledging that neuroscience has proved that people buy on emotion and justify with fact. And it means marketing to the problem and not your company's solution, seeing that building trust with customers comes from showing an empathetic understanding of their challenges. In other words it requires a completely different mindset to the one you probably have now, and we call it humanizing B2B.

Of course, lead generation and short-term tactical approaches are still important, because buyers want to know what your product's features are. But you have to balance this with a longer-term investment in brand, because while the former generates incremental growth, the latter creates transformational and sustainable expansion. This is the kind of change that can establish your business as the go-to choice in its category, sweeping the incumbent out of the way and enabling you to shift your revenue chart sharply northwards. (And if you're the incumbent yourself, watch out for challenger brands employing human-led marketing to take your place.) You could say that thinking of B2B marketing as being about creating leads is like thinking that the purpose of life is to breathe. Breathing is what keeps us alive, but what makes life worth living is how we feel about it.

So what gives us, Paul and James, the right to talk about the language of emotion in B2B? We've been evangelists for the cause for many years now, driven by the conviction that B2B marketing can and should be a force for good. We first met in 2001 when James joined Tidalwave, the marketing agency that Paul set up with his business partner Julian Sowerby in 1997, and which was one of the first in the UK to focus purely on the technology sector. After winning contracts with Hewlett-Packard and other major B2B technology companies, it was listed in the *Sunday Times* Fast Track league tables as the fastest-growing marketing agency in the UK. Paul and Julian were invited to lunch with Richard Branson, turned down an offer of £19 million for the company (what were they thinking?) and grew the business exponentially. However, it was too good to last, and when the dotcom bubble burst, they learned a series of bitter lessons in managing through a recession.

Paul and Julian eventually sold Tidalwave, and Paul set about building his current agency, Rooster Punk. It was founded with the express purpose of trying to humanize the B2B sector by bringing in new techniques such as storytelling and emotion-led marketing. In the early days this was achieved by working on brand-led projects for venture capital-funded early-stage and scale-up companies such as Funding Circle and Currencycloud, both of which are now unicorns in their respective sectors.

In the meanwhile, James had been running well-regarded tech agency Mason Zimbler, which had won B2B's Agency of the Year Award and had grown to almost 200 people across several countries. He was listed on The Drum's list of influential marketers outside London, was running a number of subsidiaries and was living the high life while racking up the proverbial air miles. However, he knew it wasn't in his DNA to chase money and status, and he felt increasingly at odds with the values his activist parents had originally instilled in him. Both men realized that they felt strongly about creating a purpose-based agency, so they joined forces and now run Rooster Punk together. That's us!

Our purpose is to humanize B2B marketing, and it's one that's enabled us to work with some remarkable marketing visionaries and business leaders who want to develop brands that matter. Our outlook is based on building human connections between companies, their employees and their customers. We've helped some businesses to double their turnovers and win awards as a result. To us, it's simply not good enough that people couldn't care less if 74% of the world's most popular brands didn't exist, as a recent survey showed;[2] B2B deserves better than this and we all need to step up to the plate to deliver it.

This has led us to create a five-point manifesto for what humanizing B2B entails.

o Be experts in people, emotion and storytelling and not just in the big tactics of B2B marketing.

o Become a trusted educator for your customers, learn for yourself and experiment.

o Understand that marketing is the mobilizer – the driver of growth and the part of the business that can build an ecosystem between HR and sales, between sales and the customer, and between marketing and the CEO and CFO – because B2B marketing means creating an environment that allows your business to fulfil its potential for all of its stakeholders: staff, customers and society as a whole.

o Have fun and rediscover the enjoyment to be found in B2B marketing.

o Leave B2B marketing in a better shape than you found it in, ready for the next generation.

This is the approach we took when we revolutionized the way that Samsung handled its B2B marketing, and it's a great story to illustrate what we mean by the power of humanizing B2B. It began when we were asked to pitch for the account. We were only a small agency at the time, and although it was an exciting piece of business to be going for we didn't want to overwhelm ourselves. The

---

[2] Beg, S. (2019). 'Havas Group's Maria Garrido Shares the Highlights of the 2019 Meaningful Brands Study and Why Being Meaningful is Good for Business', Havas Group, 26 February. https://dare.havas.com/posts/meaningful-matters/

brief contained four elements, so we chose to go for just one of them, which was to market its S7 smartphone, a device the company sold to small and medium-sized businesses in the UK.

The brief was based on the technical superiority of the Samsung phone versus the competition. We could see it was an excellent product; it was waterproof to several metres, the Gorilla® Glass was thicker and more durable than on an iPhone and the battery life was significantly longer. However, despite these advantages, we also knew that people have a love affair with Apple that transcends any of its product features. If we went for a straightforward 'look at this phone, it performs better' approach, no one would care. We instinctively knew that we needed to find a human and emotive angle if we were to win the hearts and minds of business owners.

When we sat down to work out our strategy, we reflected on the fact that we'd been iPhone users ourselves for years and had frequently felt frustrated by the deficiencies of the device. We were always wanting to make calls on the way home from work only to discover the battery had died, or visiting repair shops to have the glass replaced after dropping the phone or spilling a drink on it. What emotional effect did this have on us? It gave us the feeling of having had a bad day at work. So we created a campaign called 'More Good Days'. The thinking behind it was that when you return from work and your children ask you, 'Daddy, Daddy, did you have a good day?', your answer is often based on whether or not technology has failed you at a critical point – especially on your way home. If you ran out of battery and weren't able to make a business call on the train, it was a bad day. Our idea was that Samsung could own the feeling of having had a good day at work, and through that, talk about the features in an emotional context. It was a risky approach for us to take because we knew it would be different, but we figured we were outsiders anyway, so what did we have to lose?

We were pretty nervous when we walked into the pitch meeting and saw five or six poker-faced suits around the table, so we cut to the chase and played a 'mood-setter' video to introduce our concept. It began with some upbeat music and showed images that were relevant to the points we were putting across.

Remember how it feels to have a good day at the office? When, for the first time in ages, you get home early from work and the kids go crazy? When your inbox is under your control and the monthly sales are on-track?

After setting the scene, we introduced the problem that Samsung was solving.

Why is it these moments have become so rare? Why is it that a bad day at the office seems more common than ever? At Samsung, we're on a mission to bring about more of the good days and less of the bad.

We then went on to talk about the product features and how they benefited the user. The crucial part of this, though, was the following segment.

Why? Because it can make the difference between having a good day at the office or not. At Samsung, our technology is designed to create more good days at work. And if you're having more good days because you moved to Samsung, just think how much better your company would be if all your employees felt the same way. Let's kick the bad days into touch.

As the video progressed we could feel the energy in the room start to shift. There was a palpable move from lethargy and cynicism to positivity, and we could see that although the suits were trying to stay poker-faced they were becoming affected by what they saw. B2B marketers rarely watch an emotive video that puts their company at the heart of a story, so it must have been an empowering experience for them. Three days later we received a call: 'We want you to take on all the work, not just the part you pitched for. We believe in this new approach – it's going to be an exciting new world.' We took a deep breath, and said yes.

To cut a long story short, as a result of the work we did with Samsung, the brand won Best SMB Campaign at the B2B Marketing Awards and also smashed its sales targets. The most interesting outcome was seen in the company's partnership with Vodafone. We created a 'More Good Days' script for its sales agents so they could have a different type of conversation with business owners when they called up to introduce the S7. Instead of saying, 'Do you want a cheaper tariff?', they asked, 'Did you have a good day?' By changing the style and content of these conversations, Vodafone saw a 53% increase in its sales, simply by putting the human into the heart of its selling.

How this book will help you

We've written this book to bring the different aspects of humanized B2B marketing into one place. We recognize that not all B2B businesses are the same; at one end of the spectrum there's the owner-managed company, and at the other a major enterprise with a stakeholder buying group of ten people. What they all have in common, however, is that they want to grow, dominate their category and become meaningful. As do you.

In Part I we explain why what you're doing now isn't working well enough, and why human is the way to go. In Part II we dive into the nuts-and-bolts of a human approach to B2B, starting with how our brains function and then moving onto an explanation of the main principles of emotion-led marketing. After that, we explore the key concepts of storytelling and likeability, before rounding off with an examination of the research and data that back up everything you've learned. Being honest, we could have written a whole book on storytelling or behavioural psychology alone, but we want you to have a joined-up view of the overall subject of humanizing B2B marketing because there's something about seeing all the elements in one place that enables them to make sense.

What results can you expect from what you'll learn? That's partly up to you, but what we hope is that you'll feel a keen sense of mission. We all have a responsibility to leave B2B in a better place than we found it in, so the next generation can see this field as an aspirational and exciting place to be – the go-to sector for the brightest and best talents in marketing. This is a wake-up call for everyone currently earning a living in B2B-Land, because we all deserve to gain more, but we have to give it first.

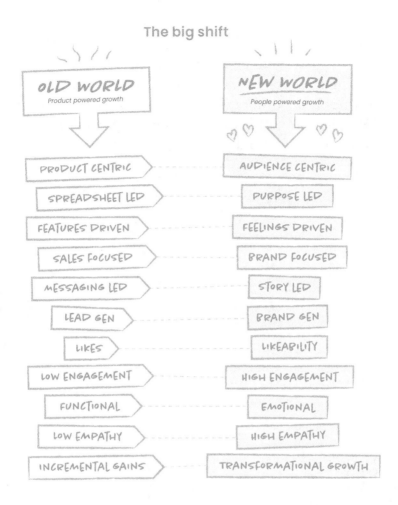

The big shift

OLD WORLD
Product powered growth

NEW WORLD
People powered growth

PRODUCT CENTRIC	AUDIENCE CENTRIC
SPREADSHEET LED	PURPOSE LED
FEATURES DRIVEN	FEELINGS DRIVEN
SALES FOCUSED	BRAND FOCUSED
MESSAGING LED	STORY LED
LEAD GEN	BRAND GEN
LIKES	LIKEABILITY
LOW ENGAGEMENT	HIGH ENGAGEMENT
FUNCTIONAL	EMOTIONAL
LOW EMPATHY	HIGH EMPATHY
INCREMENTAL GAINS	TRANSFORMATIONAL GROWTH

New world, old world
© Rooster Punk 2021

We wrote this book during the COVID-19 pandemic, which has been an interesting time, to say the least. Although little in life is certain at the best of times, let alone now, something we can be sure of is that every crisis brings change; old business models die and new ones are born. There's never been a better time for B2B marketing to become the growth engine for ambitious brands. It won't be easy – it will require courage, character and self-belief – but it will be worth it if we can create a 'new normal' for B2B. One that focuses on feelings, not just features; on storytelling, not just messaging; and on likeability, not just likes. For you to be part of this, you need information and insights, so let's dive in.

Part I
Why B2B marketing has to change

What you're doing isn't working

Telling you that what you're doing isn't working seems like a pretty bold statement, and we'd not be surprised if you found yourself disagreeing with it. 'What do you mean, not working? If I reduce my prices, it increases revenue. When I invest in advertising, new leads come in. And the last time we revamped our search engine optimization (SEO), we climbed up the rankings. Sure, some campaigns have been more successful than others, but they certainly work.'

Let's be clear: we're not saying that what you're doing isn't triggering any results. The problem is that those results are *incremental* increases in marketing KPIs and, if you're lucky, pipeline and sales. They keep you going, but they don't put you in the category's number-one spot or entrench you there forever. If you're like most B2B businesses, your marketing has been stuck in a rut for as long as you can remember; you treat business buyers and decision makers as driven purely by logic and reason, and there's little humanity or emotion in your communications. This has become a dogma in B2B

Land, so ingrained in its thinking that it's become almost impossible to imagine anything different.

How did B2B marketing become this way? Was there one particular morning when we strode into the office, took off our personalities, along with our coats, and morphed into robots? And even if there was, what on earth made us think it was a good idea? Of course it didn't happen quite like that, but at some point B2B marketers must have collectively decided that a logical, binary way of approaching marketing made sense. Maybe the engineers, scientists and technologists who made up the majority of B2B preferred it like that, and assumed everyone else did too. Or maybe it was just easier that way.

If we're to dig ourselves out of this mess, we need to understand what went wrong, because it wasn't always like this. Back in the 1970s and even into the early 1990s, B2B marketing (then called 'industrial marketing') was mainly carried out through trade catalogues, events and sometimes direct mail. It offered some interesting and effective ways of connecting with customers, especially on the advertising front, and tried to be solution-focused. Some of it had a deeply human element.

So what changed? In the late 1990s, the Internet burst onto the scene and changed our world. Although, to be more accurate, it wasn't its arrival that made the difference to B2B marketing, but marketers' knee-jerk reaction to it. Suddenly our industry was handed a whole new way of communicating its products to buyers, and we had no time to adjust to it – we just grabbed it with both hands and ran with it.

Imagine (or remember) that time; companies like Vodafone, Oracle and Microsoft were just starting to promote themselves in a significant way. The personal computer became a thing, along with mobile phones and their accompanying networks, to say nothing of in-house company databases and enterprise software packages. It was all brand-new, and it needed to be explained to the people who these companies wanted to buy it. But how to use this new tool called the Internet to do the explaining? What was it for? How did it work? The easiest answer was to reduce everything down to 'speeds and feeds', or features and – if we were lucky – benefits. Technology products made up a new category which demanded its own rules: put a picture of a router or PC on a website, list what it does, splash a price point alongside it (easily tweaked for those all-important offers) and – boom – people will buy. The last thing anyone thought about was how to engage audiences or develop brands; they were too busy focusing on promoting their product's specific technology advantage.

To be fair, it worked for a while because buyers *did* want to know how many megabytes a broadband service offered or what price a PC manufacturer was charging for the basic compared to the enhanced version. It made sense, even if it was binary and unimaginative, and we can see the same early-market-stage thinking today with cutting-edge technology such as AI. The problem with it emerged as technology advanced, with competitors playing an ever-quicker game of catch-up so that the majority of the products at similar price points were almost identical to one another.

In most B2B markets there's historically been one driver of value. Mobile phones used to be promoted according to how many megapixels they had: 8, 10, 12 or 16. Eventually the megapixels climbed to dizzying heights of 18 and we stopped caring how many there were – it became meaningless. What could possibly be the difference between 16 and 18? It was the same with broadband. In the beginning we'd dial up a 16KB connection, then were offered 256KB, then 1MB, then 2MB, then 6MB. Today we have 'high-speed broadband' and we don't even know what it is. The value drivers have become standardized, giving buyers the same lack of reason – in terms of features – to buy one brand over another as the consumer market has faced for years in the form of homogeneous products like lager and bottled water. Consumer marketers, of course, have long risen to this challenge by creating brands that tap into people's emotions as a way of generating loyalty, but not so in B2B.

Another factor in the de-humanizing of B2B was the development of 'software as a service' (SaaS). To appreciate the scale of the change this brought, cast your mind back to (or imagine) when a customer relationship management (CRM) database was something every large enterprise had to have. Software providers such as Oracle would install complex CRM programmes on company servers at vast expense, and they'd need maintaining by companies' IT departments. One day, newcomer Salesforce disrupted the market by providing the same database facility but hosted in the cloud, so the data could be accessed from anywhere. The system needed no updating or maintenance, and was paid for by a flexible subscription that could be cancelled at any time.

Services like these surged in popularity and are now used by businesses of all sizes. This has been a win for many, but has also eroded the role of the traditional sales person – the human face of the software provider. Sure, those guys (and they were almost always guys) were pricey, with their company cars and expense accounts, but they were also pretty amazing at building relationships with buyers – to the point at which if they left for another company, they'd often take their willing clients with them. However, the efficiency of the SaaS model dictated that sales teams be slashed in favour of encouraging businesses to sign up to software services online. This was another nail in the coffin of the emotional connection between B2B seller and buyer.

So we can see how the transition from industrial marketing to B2B marketing was generated by the explosion of new technology, both in terms of the products that needed to be sold and the main vehicle through which they could be promoted: the Internet. All of a sudden, marketers were able to reach customers at scale. We had email – we could spam people! We had banner ads – we could distract people! Some of it worked, and still does, but this opening up of a brave new world of mass communication made us lazy. It was fast-food marketing, with messages aimed at the lowest common denominator in a way that our B2C colleagues have always found inexplicable.

Pulling levers

We understand how we got here, but what's going on now? If you look around you, we're willing to bet you see something like this. You've ended up mired in the 'dreaded *ers*': customers wanting products that are quick*er*, cheap*er* or smart*er* than what they've currently got. They don't want anything more meaningful than that because you've never offered it, forgetting that it's your responsibility to excite them and serve them beyond their expectations, not just to give them what they ask for.

Simply focusing on promoting how your service will improve on what was there before means that you spend your time pulling levers. Each lever represents a tactic you can deploy, whether it be creating social media posts, placing ads online, revamping your website or sending email campaigns. They give sales a short-term boost but they're so boring and limited, aren't they? They don't engage with your audience on a higher level or create any meaningful loyalty to your brand. Instead, they encourage you to keep focusing on numbers so you can manipulate your figures to prove you've done the right thing.

This is understandable given the pressure on you to deliver results, but when you spend your time reporting on pointless KPIs such as bounce rates, conversion rates and costs per click, as opposed to meaningful outcomes such as increased win rates against your competitors and long-term sales, you'll stay stuck. As Jan Gladziejewski, VP Regional Marketing and Communication at DXC Technology, said to us, 'I've never seen a CEO who's really interested in a set of marketing KPIs. We need to be brutal about what's relevant to the C-suite.' Occasionally a shiny new tactic such as influencer marketing will come along, waving temptingly at you from your Instagram feed, and you'll chase it to achieve a better *this* or a better *that* (the *ers* again). You'll win a little and that will make you feel good, but you won't win big. You won't want to risk what you already have, which is – let's face it – not too bad.

The market is changing and has been for some time. Millennials, with their relative openness to the value of emotion in business, are now in positions of buying power. An increasing number of women work in senior positions, either in companies or as founders and entrepreneurs of sizeable businesses; they have more of a practised understanding of how empathy is baked into our human experience and how it influences our buying decisions. The median age of people in the UK and Europe is now over 40 for the first time ever, with the USA catching up quickly. We are an ageing population, and as we grow older we naturally become less interested in ourselves and more focused on family, legacy and the planet. This combination of changes means the B2B buyers who are now in their 40s and 50s are more broad-minded and compassionate than they were 20 years ago, with their younger counterparts just coming into the workplace being equally so.

There's also been a revolution in business thinking in recent years. The impact of Simon Sinek and his 'Start with Why' philosophy has led some boardrooms to become part of what's been called the purpose revolution. This is an emotional space that prompts leaders to question the primary reason for their company's existence – what is it they're trying to achieve, and why should this matter to their customers and employees? What social issues do they want to take a stand on, and what corresponding approach do they want their marketers to take? Add to this the new wave of conscious capitalism, in which businesses consider the environment to be one of their stakeholders, and there's a perfect melting pot of mindfulness and empathy that makes now an essential time to be more human in B2B. Increasingly, it doesn't feel right to do things the old way. And yet B2B marketing hasn't moved with the times because it doesn't want to – it prefers to stick with pulling the same old levers. That's what has to change.

How does this play out on a practical level? In our experience, most B2B buyers or decision makers live in a constant state of FEAR.[1] It's not just fear in the normal sense of the word, but fear made up of frustration, evasiveness, apathy and risk aversion. The first rule of successful marketing is to recognize this condition in the people you're selling to. Here's how it works.

o Frustration. B2B buyers and decision makers feel constantly frustrated. They're being asked to do more with less, their teams lack the skills they'd ideally like them to have and they feel overworked and underappreciated.

o Evasiveness. Because they feel hounded by marketers and sales people, they've evolved various clever ways to make themselves invisible. They use adblockers to protect their privacy, they don't answer their phones unless they have to and they long ago became blind to the banner and display ads flashing at the sides of their screens.

o Apathy. B2B buyers and decision makers have learned to ignore the vendors who claim they can transform their businesses and save them millions. They've become weary of product feature and benefit marketing, and are bombarded with so much

[1] Cash, P. (2017). 'Why are B2B Tech Buyers Living in Fear?', LinkedIn, 20 September. www.linkedin.com/pulse/b2b-tech-buyers-living-fear-paul-cash-/

content that it's a full-time job just to keep on top of the research. They feel burned-out.

o   Risk aversion. With the amount of data and information available now for research, they care more about making the wrong decision than the right one – otherwise known as loss aversion bias. As marketing luminary Rory Sutherland often points out, they're more afraid of being blamed than they are of even just getting it wrong. Added to this is the fact that many businesses now have formal buying groups or committees, which hobble buyers' independence and force them to justify every decision they make.

You can see how in this buyer and decision maker FEAR zone, if any business wins, it's the incumbent supplier because it's already 'in'. Often it leads to paralysis when no decision is made. If all you're doing as a marketer is bombarding these people with information without saying anything different or being interesting and engaging, you'll be exacerbating the FEAR by encouraging decision making paralysis rather than attracting people to your product.

What's the solution? To make decision makers feel BRAVE again. We'll be expanding on these concepts more throughout the book, but to give you a feel for how it works, BRAVE is the antidote to FEAR. At its heart is a more human-centred recognition of the drivers that affect people's decisions, and those who embrace it are – in our experience – infinitely more successful than those who stick with pulling levers.

o   Buyer emotion. People buy using their feelings and only justify their decisions with logic – pure rationality is not the main driver. If all you have is reason to bring them to you, you've missed the primary instigator of their purchase.

o Recognition. Buyers are human just like anyone else; they want to be rewarded and recognized for their work. How can you help to elevate them and their careers by enabling recognition from their teams, companies or even industries? What can you do for them, rather than asking what they can do for you? How can you make them look good so they feel good about themselves, and by extension about you?

o Appreciation. B2B buyers are coping with more technological change than practically anyone else around. But they're also human, and the pace at which they can manage this change is governed more by the limitations of human nature than by the timetable of Moore's Law. What they appreciate more than anything is suppliers who show they appreciate the challenges they face. How can you do this?

o Value. Buyers don't want hype; they want suppliers who approach them in a human, intelligent way. What could you provide that's useful to them? What value can you bring that's unique to you and different to what they could access elsewhere? Even better, think about how you can address their unconscious needs. Because the gold in the value you offer is when you teach them about a problem they didn't know they had – the one that's *not* keeping them up at night but should be. Challenge them, don't just agree with what they think they want. And don't simply solve problems; find them.

o Engagement. Buyers have high expectations of marketing – they don't want to be sold to. They're looking for you to engage them in creative and empathetic ways, because people buy human stories as much as they buy products.

You can see that the BRAVE methodology is a recognition of individual buyer emotions. You may wonder how you can cater for this when you have many accounts to manage, but here's where account-based marketing (ABM) comes in. If, like most businesses, you gain 80% of your revenue from 20% of your customers, your job is to identify the small number of buyers who make up your prime customer set. You need to understand them well enough so you can market to them one-to-one, or at least one-to-few. This way you can afford to spend the time needed to address the FEAR.

If you don't do this – if all you do is mass market to the lowest common denominator – you'll only gain the customers you deserve. The ones who moan about the price and tell you they can buy better features elsewhere. The hagglers, the switchers, the churners. They demand as much support, if not more, than the good customers, and they're attracted by speeds and feeds combined with low prices like moths to a flame. Most B2B businesses are indiscriminate about the customers they chase because they're so focused on numbers, but if you do this you'll overlook the good ones. They're the loyal customers who want to buy more than one product from you and stay even if you're more costly than the competition. They tell their peers what an amazing company you are, because they've bought into you and the value you stand for in the marketplace. And why have they done that? Because they're emotionally attached to you.

You can see from this that the most significant movement in B2B marketing of recent years is the increasing recognition that people buy on emotion, not logic. However, don't take our word for it; consider what one of the most successful B2B companies in the world has to say about it. In 2016, Google and CEB carried out a piece of seminal research called 'From Promotion to Emotion'.[2] It analyses the results of survey responses from 3,000 buyers of 36 B2B brands across multiple categories, interviews with 50 B2B leaders, and a variety of secondary research. It examines the role of emotion in the B2B sales process, along with research company Motista and CEB's Marketing Leadership Council.

The results it returns show that – contrary to expectations – a greater proportion of B2B customers are emotionally attached to a brand they've bought than they are to B2C brands. If you think about it, it's not so surprising because B2B purchases involve more personal risk. If a buyer makes the wrong choice the best that could happen is that they waste a load of time and effort, and the worst is that they lose their credibility or even their job. The desire to avoid this is a powerful one, as loss aversion theory attests; given the choice between avoiding risking a bad reputation and possibly gaining a good one, we go for the first option every time. It's no wonder that B2B decision makers feel emotional about what they buy.

Consumer marketing got its head around the importance of emotion years ago. Admittedly, it's easier to judge the results in that space, because if Unilever places a TV spot it can see the relevant products flying off the shelves the

[2] CEB in partnership with Google (2016). 'From Promotion to Emotion: Connecting B2B Customers to Brands'. https://plan2brand.com/wp-content/uploads/2015/07/CEB_Promotion_to_Emotion_whitepaper.pdf

next day. It's trickier in B2B because of the longer sales cycles, which can take anything up to a couple of years. But enough of the excuses. We can't deny that we've stuck our heads in the sand for too long, and it hasn't been entirely down to B2B buyers and decision makers – it's partly B2B agencies' responsibility too. Agencies need to find ways of showing (sometimes) sceptical clients practical ways of building humanity and emotion into their products, so they can create a brand their customers can buy into. It's like making a cake. B2B marketing is highly skilled at making cakes that look delicious, but when the customer bites into them they spit them out in disgust because marketing didn't put the sugar in. The missing sugar is the emotion, and we have to learn how to add it in, because the wonderful taste is what buyers really want.

Where do we go from here?

If you're the market leader in your category, you may be happy just pulling levers. And you're extra happy if everyone else is copying what you do, because you know they'll never overtake you. What might be keeping you up at night occasionally, though, is the thought of the number-four or number-five in your category redefining it by revolutionizing its marketing in a human way. That alone should give you pause for thought.

The good news is, if you see yourself as a change agent, a disruptor or an innovator, the prize for the taking is huge. Because if your vision is to transform your company's position in its industry, B2B is a career-defining place to do it. In fact, due to the inertia in this space, or maybe as a result of it, the industry hasn't done enough to attract people who want to make a difference. Many tech companies recruit CMOs from consumer organizations with a fanfare about it being a brave new world of brand building, but, crushed by the hostile politics of established leaders who just want things to go back to normal, the CMOs rarely last longer than a year. Let's face it, B2B is tough. It requires deep intellectual rigour and it's not for everyone. As one client recently reminded me, B2B is like chess and B2C is like draughts. I kind of like that analogy.

To counter this, there's a promising development in B2B-Land in the form of the newly created roles of chief revenue officer (CRO) and chief growth officer (CGO). This is mainly a US initiative but is making its way over to the UK, and it has vast appeal to sales or marketing directors who have their eventual sights set on the boardroom. It involves overseeing all customer-based activity, from brand, to sales, to product experience, and is exciting because the future of marketing surely has to be that everything it does is focused on growing the business. This is an opportunity for any B2B marketer to show that marketing can step up to the plate and be its own growth-driver, championing the voice of the customer and challenging the age-old dominance of the sales function.

It's also encouraging to see that B2B marketers are at long last starting to talk about the customer in terms other than numerical. The concept of customer centricity, often expressed in the hiring of well-paid customer experience managers, is the number-one or number-two priority on the agenda of many CEOs and CMOs. Perhaps it should always have been, but there we are. There's a recognition that the product-focused world of

B2B needs reinventing, and that putting the customer at the heart of product development decisions is not a 'nice to have' but an essential way of working. This hasn't fully filtered through to marketing decisions, or not nearly as much as it should have done, but at least the recognition is there. In the same way, many SaaS companies have created a new role of customer success manager (CSM), to ensure that users of their services receive the best experience possible and don't click away to a competitor. The CSM's role is to keep customers happy by focusing on their experience rather than numbers, but the problem for marketers is that – as Martin Pitcock, Head of Commercial Excellence, Ecommerce at nets points out – 'the customer success teams don't report into marketing. We still have some way to go if we want to put marketing into the centre of business growth.'

We speak to some companies that have given 'brand stuff' a try and found it didn't work. However, when we ask them about what they actually did, it turns out it was rarely a brand campaign in the true sense but more of an enhanced lead generation effort. It takes time and resources to build a human brand – it's not something you can achieve with a one-off campaign. Branding is a long-term game and you need a long-term mindset to give yourself the chance to succeed. We know that's hard, because you could gain short-term results more quickly and be able to justify the results at the next quarterly review. It's tough to bet on the future, but that's the crux of it. Surely the reason you went into marketing in the first place was to show that, through a blend of creativity and hard-nosed business sense, you could take your company in a new direction, and through that create revenues it's never seen before? Marketing needs more of that approach, not countless people pulling the same levers at different times.

There's been talk of the lack of emotion in B2B marketing for a decade – it's not a new story. It's just that, for some reason, marketers haven't been sure how to use it and B2B agencies haven't done a good enough job of explaining it. Now is the time to change. If you're to dodge the meteor heading your way, your marketing needs to put your customers into the heart of the conversation you have with them. What this will entail is the topic we'll be starting to explore in the next chapter.

Key takeaways

o   In the beginning, B2B marketing integrated emotion into its thinking as a natural part of what it did.
o   When products became more technical and were increasingly sold online, manufacturers moved to selling features rather than feelings.
o   Using short-term, tactical means to market products produces mediocre results.
o   Times have changed, and B2B buyers want to feel emotionally connected to what they buy. This is backed up by research.

The new truth

There's a new age dawning in B2B marketing, and it's powered by what we call 'the new truth'. This truth is that people don't want to buy *from* you, they want to buy *into* you; they want to know what your company stands for, why it exists and what kind of people are behind it. They want to see its human face – in other words, its brand.

There's another truth as well, which is that if you believe in the above you'll find it impossible to be satisfied any longer with the binary world of features-led B2B marketing. It will seem limited, grey and stale. You'll look around and wonder how you accepted it for so long and why other people still do. Put another way, if you don't embrace this new mindset you'll become extinct and the meteor will have won. So we're going to be completely honest and tell you that this book will be of *no* use to you if you:

o think that the best product always wins
o assume that the more leads you have, the more products you'll sell

o think that buyers and decision makers are initially attracted to products because they have the best features

o reckon a brand is something you can create after you've generated enough sales

o enjoy poring over sales data showing your latest 1% increase

o are convinced that you buy everything for logical reasons

There's no middle ground here; you're either in or you're out. If your mindset is locked into the idea that people just want to buy your product, you'll eventually die out. If it's expansive enough to understand that they want to buy into your brand instead (even if you're not quite sure how that works yet), you'll prosper. As Mark Bogaerts, Director of Brand and Sponsorship at Tata Consulting Services, said to us, 'B2C is driven by brand and B2B is driven by sales.' The shift from sales to brand is everything, and challenging your current thinking is the first step in your journey of brand discovery.

If you're not yet sure what your mindset is, ask yourself this: 'When I think about pulling marketing levers, do I feel happy? Do I feel excited? Can I see the potential in it?' If the answer is 'no' or even 'maybe not', you need to be brave and aim higher because there's another, much more powerful lever called 'brand'. If you pull that one well, adjusting the others alongside it will have a magnified effect. Think of it as a master lever; not only will it position you for long-term sales in its own right, but your lead generation will receive more traction, your product enhancements will gain more attention and your social media will attract more eyeballs. These are the results that a brand mindset can bring.

Why now?

As we write, the world is in the grip of the COVID-19 pandemic and whole nations are in lockdown. This has triggered a wave of responses from companies, many of them designed to help people in their hour of need – in fact, consumers are crying out for information and support. Research by Ipsos[1] shows that 74% of people want to hear from helpful brands, and almost as many think that businesses have a social responsibility to offer aid during the crisis. It therefore makes sense for those businesses to provide that support, because after the world has emerged from this it won't go back to the way it was. History teaches us that post-crisis periods are always characterized by intense technological progress and a re-casting of our ideas about how we relate to one another and the world. Now is no different, in that our unchanging human desires – for self-expression, belonging, acceptance, knowledge, communication and self-fulfilment – will continue to drive our decisions. Companies that prove their worth when the chips are down will be valued long into the future.

Certain firms are stepping up to the plate. In the USA, Ford has replaced its product ads with alternatives reassuring customers it will pause their credit payments; when asked what they thought of the company after seeing the campaign, 90% of people agreed that Ford was 'an important part of American culture'. Let that sink in – a brand embedding itself into the national psyche during its darkest hour. Imagine what an impact that will have on Ford's long-term viability.

---

[1] Sheridan, A., Debia, A., Tian, L., Franke, L. and Rodgers, R. (2020). 'COVID-19: The Creative Fightback'. Ipsos MORI. www.ipsos.com/ipsos-mori/en-uk/covid-19-creative-fightback

Of course, well before the current crisis, it was clear there was no longer any such thing as business as usual. This is a notion that Simon Sinek expresses eloquently in his description of the new organizational world as being an 'infinite game'. A 'finite game' is about beating the competition using unchanging rules. One company launches a new product feature, only to be trounced by a competitor launching a better version of the same feature. Customers switch from the first company to the second, leading the first to lower its price... and we know how the story goes from there.

In an infinite game, on the other hand, new rules and players can enter at any time, leading to a situation in which no one business ever 'wins', but carries on playing and innovating forever. In this world we don't know what's going to happen next, but we do know that if we have a solid brand to carry us through we won't have to resort to a continuous stream of discounts and dry product offers. Now more than ever, the companies that have invested in their brands and have a strong purpose are the ones that will thrive regardless of the circumstances. Ford didn't win people over by launching a car with a new feature; it did it by addressing its customers' collective emotional state in a positive and constructive way.

As we saw in the last chapter, what's also evolved is the increasing disengagement of business decision makers from marketing. Because of the way they've been marketed to for the past 20 years, they're feeling frustrated, evasive, apathetic and risk-averse, and are sick of being bombarded with fact-based content. Why do they need it from brands in any case? They can go online and discover the data for themselves. Research shows that B2B buyers are more than 70% of the way through their decision making process before they even pick up the phone to speak to a supplier; with all the content on the B2Bi @ LinkedIn, social media and blog posts, they're informing themselves in a way that suits them, ahead of time.[2] If all they receive when they speak to you is more of the same, you'll never be in the competitive frame. We know what a challenge it can be for marketers to resist the pull of data-focused content, because it's so prevalent now. Nick Ashmore, VP of Marketing at ResponseTap, acknowledges this: 'Fighting against meaningless content and general marketing churn is a constant battle.' The thing is, you have to do it.

Ironically, one of the consistencies of human nature is our resistance to change – our innate tendency towards scepticism and negativity when confronted with something new. But what if the need to change wasn't a problem? What if it could be fun, exciting, revealing and intriguing? This unstable state of affairs creates a new paradigm for B2B marketing, in which constant innovation and customer engagement has become more than a canny strategy for ambitious, upwardly mobile companies – it's become an absolute necessity for survival. A relatively consistent and predictable world, in which market leaders enjoyed economies of scale and achieved dominance over smaller rivals, has long given way to a more unpredictable environment in which dominant market 'gorillas' are increasingly vulnerable to the guerrilla strategies of faster, more creative opponents.

---

[2] Erskine, R. (2017). 'How To Turn B2B Buyers Into Sales Leads, According To Data', *Forbes*, 28 December. www.forbes.com/ sites/ryanerskine/2017/12/28/how-to-turn-b2b-buyers-into-sales-leads-according-to-data

The five principles of growth in B2B

In 2019, the B2B Institute at LinkedIn (B2Bi @ LinkedIn), frustrated with the paucity of research material on B2B brand building, commissioned brand effectiveness luminaries Les Binet and Peter Field to carry out original research on the fundamentals of B2B marketing. Surely, thought the B2Bi @ LinkedIn, we instinctively know that we buy from brands rather than faceless companies, so why wasn't there more evidence-based research on the subject? And why did B2B not seem to understand the long-term value of brands? To answer this, Binet and Field used the UK IPA Databank, one of the world's best sources of information on marketing effectiveness, to see which B2C and B2B strategies worked best. They discovered some interesting patterns in the data which show that B2B has much to learn from B2C. If you want more of a nuts-and-bolts rundown of the research, you'll find it later in the chapter 'The undeniable facts'; what follows is a useful summary to get you thinking.

The resulting report[3] is a goldmine of information which, in our view, is essential reading for any B2B marketer wanting to transform their company's fortunes. In summary, it shows that 'a number of key growth drivers in B2C marketing also work for B2B businesses, and by implication that there is a much greater commonality in best practice across B2C and B2B sectors than is usually believed', which is just a somewhat dry way of advising B2B marketers to learn from consumer brands

[3] Binet, L. and Field, P. (2019). 'The 5 Principles of Growth in B2B Marketing: Empirical Observations on B2B Effectiveness', The B2B Institute and LinkedIn. https://business.linkedin.com/marketing-solutions/b2b-institute/marketing-as-growth

if they want to transform their sales and position their companies as the 'go-tos' in their categories.

The key outcome of the research is what it called the five principles of B2B marketing.

1. Invest in share of voice. B2B brands that invest in their share of voice tend to grow, whereas those that do the opposite tend to shrink. The logical follow-on from this is that you need to talk to more customers than you currently have in order to expand your sales. What they're really talking about here is brand advertising.

2. Balance brand and activation activity. Tactical activation campaigns can produce high ROI but they're not likely to be very memorable, their effects are short-lived and they do little to foster long-term growth. In contrast, brand building is ideal for lifelong growth, because it works emotionally to create associations that influence purchase decisions long after the campaign ends. This requires a much broader reach than tactical marketing, but it's ultimately more effective because it lasts for longer and the impact accumulates over time. Brand building also reduces price sensitivity and therefore allows you to increase margins, which is why it's the main driver of long-term growth and profits. The practical outcome of this is that B2B brands should balance their budgets between long-term brand building and short-term sales activation with roughly a 50:50 split. This is not what happens now.

3. Expand your customer base. Although you might assume that gaining new customers is of equal

value to selling more to existing ones (and even that
the latter is more profitable because recruiting new
customers is expensive), the data shows that this
is not the case. In fact, B2B customer acquisition
strategies are more effective than loyalty strategies;
in other words, you grow by targeting *new* customers
and *not* existing ones. This means that the most
successful B2B brands are the ones that 'have the
most customers, and they tend to be the brands
that talk to most people in the market, most often'.
You can't do this if you limit yourself to prospect
outreach on a one-to-one basis, alongside the odd
email campaign to your existing customers.

4. Maximize mental availability. Although most
people realize how important mental availability
is in B2C marketing (we buy the brands we know
the best because it's easier), it's often assumed
not to matter so much in B2B. Marketers think
that B2B buyers take a logical and considered
approach to purchase decisions, preferring to go
with the product with the most relevant features
rather than the brand they feel most affinity
with. However, Binet and Field give the famous
example of the saying that first took hold in the
1970s: 'No-one ever got fired for buying IBM'.
This exploited business buyers' limited mental
availability with the aim of appealing straight to
their emotions. It means that B2B campaigns that
aim to increase a company's share of mind are the
ones that work the best; the more famous they
make the brand, the better the results.

5. Harness the power of emotion. Emotional
messaging in B2B is more effective in the long

run and rational messaging in the short run. What are the implications of this? For marketing to customers who are ready to buy you should be rational, and for those who haven't yet considered your product you should be emotional. In other words, if people have already bought into you as a business they'll be open to messages containing offers and new feature information, but if they're not they need to be wooed emotionally first.

This ground-breaking report reveals how brand-led marketing is the fundamental driver of growth in your business. We feel pretty sad that it hasn't been read by many CEOs, because they'd stand a much higher chance of transforming their company fortunes if they did. What's even more frustrating is that most B2B marketers are doing the exact opposite of what's recommended in this report. Rather than committing themselves to the enduring task of building a brand, they rarely measure the impact of campaigns for longer than six months. Rather than focusing on reaching new customers, they labour under the misapprehension that businesses grow by increasing loyalty. And rather than putting their energies into brand advertising, they dismiss the notion that having an advertising presence enables them to increase their margins and therefore profits.

It sounds like a depressing scenario, and it could be if you wanted to see it that way. But, looked at from another angle, it represents a golden opportunity. Binet and Field conclude that this is the time for brave B2B marketers to be 'both right and contrarian' – to reject the consensus and 'bet big' on these principles in order to beat their competition and establish themselves as the main players in their categories.

Brand matters

Many CEOs roll their eyes at the word 'brand'. It's colouring-in, logos, pretty designs or, at best, corporate identity – all the old-fashioned things that brand used to represent. What they don't think of when they hear that word (because they don't have the brand mindset) is that brand is the key driver of growth in their companies.

And yet it shouldn't be so hard to see why brand works. We all have experience of paying more for something, or plumping quickly for it over other options, because of the way we *feel* about a business. We're happy to bet that, when buying a car, most B2B CEOs choose between a Tesla, BMW, Range Rover or another premium brand. Why would they do that, when logic suggests a cheaper marque would give as many features for their money? And what if those same CEOs were to cast their eyes over their own product lines and compare them with those of their competitors? How much differentiation would they see? There's probably not even the most basic difference between the Range Rover of financial software and the Skoda – it doesn't exist. These CEOs expect their customers to pick one over another based purely on whatever minor functional difference or price advantage it offers.

This is where the concept of mental availability comes in, as mentioned in the research by Binet and Field. We use mental shortcuts to make decisions all the time without realizing it. Which way will I drive to see a friend? The one I'm most familiar with, even if it's not the fastest. What will I do first when I get into the office – make a cup of coffee or switch on my laptop? The one I always do, because that way I don't have to decide. We love the familiar, and this is why brands advertise; if we've seen a product on our TV screens or in our social media feeds often enough, we tend to assume it's a good one to buy. We trust it. In the absence of an overwhelming reason to buy a competitor product, we drift towards the one we know. It has set up shop in our mental space and now it's selling us its wares.

If you were to adopt a brand-led approach to your products, you would see what a positive impact it would have on your marketing funnel. There's a myth in B2B that you should only market to the people in your buying frame, and yet the research says the opposite. You need to reach out to as wide an audience as possible if you want to be successful. That audience would be unlikely to fall into a typical B2B lead generation programme, because in the absence of a brand, all leads enter your funnel looking for something functional. These are not necessarily the customers you want. They've been sucked in by the seductive lure of your short-term promotions, instead of jumping in voluntarily because they already love what you stand for as a company. The stronger your brand, the more the best people will be attracted into your funnel, the more likely they are to buy from you and to love using your product, and the greater the number of others they'll recommend you to. They'll also acquire more products from you, seeing themselves as buying into your company rather than just the one widget they've already purchased. To take a

B2C example, remember when Apple launched the iPad; it was able to convince large numbers of people they needed a completely novel device that was something between a phone and a laptop, all because of trust in Apple as a brand.

The role of brand is to be a signpost that makes it easy for buyers to decide whether or not to engage with you. Once they've bought into you they'll be willing to pay a higher price than if they were only after the latest incremental feature enhancement or special offer. This allows you to pass the cost of advertising onto them via your own margins. Think of why we pay more for a Prada suit than a chain-store one; it's much the same outfit, but Prada has built a fashion brand that's valuable in the market and can therefore command a premium. For this reason alone, if not all the others, it makes terrible business sense for B2B companies to have so little ambition for their potential brands. The human truth is that decision makers want to buy into your company, which entails you investing in your brand; this is the primary driver of growth, value and equity in your business. In the absence of a brand, all you're left with is the fast-food, lead generation marketing that you've been doing for the last ten years, and that's not got you anywhere significant to date.

Sometimes it's easier to understand this through a couple of examples. Enterprise software provider SAP is doing a great job of building an emotional bridge between the company and its customers, and of differentiating itself in the process. To promote its Experience Management package, it rolled out an ad featuring actor Clive Owen humorously listing the wide range of human feelings that could be recorded and measured by it. This exploits one of B2C's classic tricks for making products more relatable and memorable, which is to make use of personalities and ambassadors; think of Nanette Newman for Fairy Liquid, or the meerkats for Compare the Market. This kind of symbolism is massively powerful because it gives consumers a character or familiar face to hang the product on; we might not remember the name of the service but we'll enter 'meerkats insurance' into Google. And B2B is no different, as the research shows.

Maersk Line, the Danish shipping conglomerate, is another great example.[4] Who would have thought that a business transporting containers around the world could build a personality? But it has, and its efforts have netted it a number of awards for its approach to social media. In 2011, it created one of the most successful content marketing strategies ever for a B2B company, which involved setting up over 30 social accounts across different markets. It chose to do this not to generate leads or bring in customers directly, but to share relevant and engaging content in the form of powerful and interesting stories. It's done a brilliant job of telling audiences about the reality of container shipping through human narratives, such as the video it created when an employee fell overboard and spent ten hours in the Atlantic before being rescued. The narrative recounts what happened through the voices of the people involved, concluding with the happy ending.

As the Binet and Field report concludes, brand advertising attracts people to buy your products by

[4] Lakhani, A. (2013). '7 Lessons for Effective B2B Content Marketing via the Maersk Line Case Study', SearchDecoder, 11 July. www.searchdecoder.com/b2b-content-marketing

creating associations between your brand, the buying occasion and the emotions that prime buyers to choose you. The advantage of this emotional approach is that it's memorable and enduring, which means that when you pull your functional marketing levers your results from them will be magnified. You'll only need to tweak them instead of giving them a heave.

Of course, rational measures such as promotions still work for short-term sales, but it's brand building that lays the foundation for long-term success. If you're able to bring customers into your business because they want to be there, you can give them the product information they need once they've crossed the threshold. In any case, they're certainly not interested in it before they've decided they like you – they'll just screen out your rational sales messages or forget them, because they're the same as everyone else's.

B2C businesses tend to follow the 60:40 rule, with emotional priming being the dominant task. The research shows that B2B businesses should use a 46:54 rule, with 46% of resource directed towards brand building and 54% towards rational activation messaging. Even though the weighting is slightly more towards the rational than the emotional, it's still very different to what most B2B marketers practise today.

The power of stories

One development that we can be pleased about is that the concept of storytelling is becoming popular in B2B-Land. Almost every CEO knows that their company needs to have a better story to tell, because they're increasingly convinced it will translate into more growth and consistency of message. In a way, emotional storytelling has become the 'new brand', and it's what many fast-growing and high-value businesses are doing. We'll be exploring the role and nature of stories more deeply later in the book, but it's worth touching on here because of the intimate relationship they have with brand building.

Storytelling is essential to our lives. Ever since the first humans sat around a campfire recounting the dangers and triumphs of their day, we've been attuned to listen to and remember stories for our very survival. Storytelling also weaves its way through Binet and Field's five principles of B2B growth. It helps businesses to increase their share of voice, enabling them to dominate the conversation in their industries; through that it enables them to expand their customer bases; it maximizes the mental availability of their brands, making the decision to buy from them more straightforward; and it captures people's imaginations.

Ask yourself: if your company had a clearer and more engaging story to tell, would you win more customers? If your sales people had a script to use that tapped into what made your brand special, would they gain more business? The answer has to be yes. So why are you only focusing on selling features and benefits? You should be competing on your story, not your products, because there's a far more powerful differentiation in your story than there is in your speeds and feeds. In all mature, competitive markets the only element that separates one company from another is brand, of which story is a key part: how businesses show up in the market, how they communicate and what kind of personalities they have. This is what we resonate with as business buyers as much as we do as consumers.

Like it or not, you have to earn the right to talk about your product before people will listen, and this means that at the beginning of developing a relationship with your customers it's more important to be interesting than it is to be right. That doesn't mean being all style and no substance, but you do have to find ways to burst through the individual bubbles that decision makers have surrounded themselves with. You won't do that by explaining your features, but you could do it by telling a compelling story. Successful brands have stories as part of their marketing DNA. Salesforce, for instance, has an internal team dedicated to telling stories about its brand, focusing on what it calls the 'Trailblazers' who are using its CRM platform to grow their businesses.[5] It doesn't see itself as simply selling a product, but as a driving force behind empowering the whole business community.

But what about your products, you may be asking yourself? Surely they're worthy of a story. Sometimes they are, but there's a huge difference between product-powered growth and people-powered growth. The former is what B2B has been doing for the past 20 years and the latter is what it should be doing now – building emotional connections between customers and brands. The strength of stories is in their humanity, and as you know by now, human is the way to go. In the next chapter you'll learn more about what it means to do B2B marketing the human way.

---

[5] Salesforce (n.d.). 'Explore All the Trailblazers Who Are Succeeding with Salesforce'. www.salesforce.com/customer-success-stories

Key takeaways

o Brand-based marketing is a mindset – if you haven't got it, learn it.

o New ways of thinking about business dictate that now is the time to change your mindset.

o B2B marketing needs to place a greater focus on brand building in order to attract the most profitable customers.

o It must also talk to as many people as possible through advertising and storytelling, thereby staking its place in customers' limited mental availability space.

o Brand building attracts willing customers to your company, turbo-charging the effect of your lead generation activity.

o Storytelling is a key part of brand building because it makes your products relatable and memorable.

Human-to-human

You'd be hard-pressed to find any business that doesn't swear on its mother's life that it puts its customers first. Of course it does. And yet, bizarrely, customers are not at the centre of most businesses. Even B2C companies have to try hard to remember that customers are the most important element of their operations, and in B2B-Land they barely get a look in. Products come first every time, and if you don't think this is true for you, please read on before you make up your mind.

Naturally, customers should be at the heart of your business, not just lucky to be considered at the end of the product development and sales process. It's no different with your marketing. B2B companies don't sell to bricks and mortar; they sell to people. It's a *person* who's at the receiving end of your marketing activity, whether they be a chief procurement officer (CPO), a chief financial officer (CFO), a chief information officer (CIO) or a managing director (MD) of a small business (those initials and job titles are a great way of dehumanizing people, aren't they?). Everything you do is aimed at a human being who has feelings, preferences and insecurities, just like you do. Of course, in B2B marketing you're speaking not to just one person but to a whole audience made up of employees and business partners. For this reason we prefer the term 'audience' to the word 'customer', although the advantage of the latter is that it helps to conjure up an image of a human being.

People are everywhere throughout any business – every company is a people-based one. Pre-Internet, all B2B marketing and sales was human-to-human, but our focus on building machines to do the same job has dehumanized B2B. The SaaS model is a classic example of this; although it offers superb efficiencies and is often favoured by customers, it's easy to forget that it also mechanizes what was once a people-based process. This means you need to spend more time, effort and money investing in the people who are the interface between your company and those who buy your products. We're talking about frontline staff, whether they be call centre agents, customer service managers or delivery drivers – all those who interact with people outside your business. And you also need to invest in your brand, because that's the other key way you can express your humanity and appeal to the human beings who you want to buy from you. It's time to redress the balance.

You may be thinking that none of this is rocket science and that there's been a background hum about moving to a more customer-led marketing model for years. You'd be right, but the problem is that most B2B businesses haven't made it happen in reality. We have to get away from this impersonal approach and engage directly with audiences on their issues and challenges – the things that are important to them in their lives. More than this, we need to use emotion to unlock people's understanding so we can move minds and thereby move products. This is what humanizing B2B is all about.

What are your customers experiencing?

Discussions about the customer experience have been circulating around B2C boardroom tables for the past five years now. From all the research we've seen, it's one of the top three elements these companies are concentrating on to increase their sales and retain the loyalty of their existing customers. The customer experience is now seen as the primary factor to consider when designing technology platforms or creating new services. In B2B, although putting customers at the centre of things was the way it was 50 years ago, now it's moved backwards. Given that there's a resurgence of interest in customers and what they want from brands in B2C, we think B2B needs to take up the people baton and run with it.

So how does B2B currently get this wrong? Suppose you work for a manufacturer of industrial printers. You have four manufacturing plants across the world, which means you need to make at least X million printers a year to break even, and your team of innovators is constantly finding ways to enhance them with new features so you can increase your sales. Along comes new printer XY24X, which can print an amazing 1,000 pages per minute (the value driver in your industry). You, the product marketing manager of this printer, need to sell X thousand units a year to make it a success, and have a multi-million marketing budget to achieve this. If you were marketing that product, what would you say about it to your potential customers? We know what the answer is. You'd focus on a unique selling point – the pages per minute – and any other technical features you can think of. You certainly wouldn't be talking about brand values or the emotional reasons people would want to buy from you.

This is how all similar companies are structured – the budget follows the product. It's like the product is a magnet, drawing resources and attention to it wherever it goes. It's rare to find a CMO in a B2B business who has the freedom to decide how marketing spend should be allocated across the whole range of products, thereby allowing them to focus on the overarching brand. Instead, attention is wired to finding new product USPs and then flogging the hell out of them. And because it's easier for these kinds of businesses to talk about products than customers, they keep being dragged around by the product magnet. It's not that many companies haven't tried to change this over the years, seeing that there should be a balance between talking about products and appealing to human emotions. But when the CEO only wants to know how many printers have been sold that quarter and at what margin, everyone's attention is drawn towards the product again.

Even SaaS companies operate this way. In a bid to be customer-focused they base their software updates on the new features their customers are asking for, but the problem is that they're not addressing the real pain their customers have. If you ask your customers what they want, they'll always give you the three *ers*: quicker, cheaper, faster. What else would they think of? Simply giving them what they've requested will never make your brand number-one. It's your responsibility to come up with the visionary ideas that will achieve that.

Be intimate with your customers but don't be led by them; don't confuse delivering what they 'want' with doing good marketing. If you treat B2B marketing as a product process – create a concept, prove it, ship it, then sell it to the markets – the customer will always be an afterthought.

Instead, if you say to yourself, 'We have these amazing customers. What can we create for them? What would inspire them? What would make us truly irresistible to them? And what kind of company do they want to buy from in any case?', think how transformational that would be. You'd be addressing their unconscious needs, which are far more powerful than their conscious ones. You want to be a teacher, not a sales person; a trusted educator, not a mere advisor. Offering new insights through your products, services and marketing is the ultimate place to be – you're irreplaceable then.

Marketing on purpose

It can be tempting to think of brand marketing as all style and no substance, and of course, if done badly, it is. But people are drawn to brands for deeper reasons than the glitter of a campaign; they want to buy into the essence of them – their 'why'. Brands that mean something to people don't win that love because of what they do or even how they do it; they're loved for *why* they do it. These companies have a sense of mission, a driving motive that goes beyond making money, selling stuff or being number-one. As Simon Sinek said, 'Profit isn't a purpose. It's a result.' Great marketers understand this, creating and communicating valuable purposes that their customers can relate to.

Having a purpose is kind of fashionable at the moment, but although many organizations are trying to hardwire purpose into what they do, few are truly walking the talk. Having a purpose entails your company showing up in the world in a way that proves you're trying to make a meaningful and positive difference to the lives of your customers, and not just selling products for the sake of it. What purpose does a printer manufacturer serve, for instance? Is it to bring people together through visual communications? To make words and images real and permanent? To enable small businesses to thrive? These deeper questions may feel uncomfortable and can seem irrelevant to your finance director, but to your customers they're important.

Although it's hard enough developing a purpose in theory, it's even more difficult to put it into practice, and this is where all the brainstorming sessions and colourful slide decks can give way to harsh reality. When a business wants to hold itself up to a higher standard it will be costly, operationally challenging and will create more work for people. It might not be able to use the same suppliers as before, or pay its operational staff as little as it can get away with. When the first couple of quarters' figures come through, the CEO might start to wonder if it's all worth it. Creating and enacting a purpose is a leadership, rather than a marketing, challenge. Marketing can be the champion for it, igniting the spark that makes people want to support it internally, but unless the business as a whole grabs hold of it and wants to turn it into something that differentiates it from its competitors, it just becomes another fail point that the CMO doesn't want to carry the can for. If you don't want a new purpose proposition to be created only for the slide decks to gather dust, it has to be led from the top.

Of course, this was never going to be easy. We've worked on over 50 purpose-driven projects over the past decade, and one thing we've learned is that the commitment of the CEO and leadership team to their purpose is everything. And it can be achieved. There are some brilliant success stories of B2B brands with a purpose that's joined-up with their product development and marketing. Peer-to-peer lender Funding Circle encourages small businesses to believe in themselves; Kickstarter brings creative projects to life; and SAP uses its technology to help the world run better and improves people's lives. As Joanne Gilhooley, Global Marketing Leader at Microsoft, puts it, 'If you get great people together, good things will happen.'

Purpose has to run through the business like a stick of rock, which is why most don't bother doing it – they'd rather not run the risk of failing. Even in B2C it's a challenge, let alone in B2B, where most CEOs simply don't get it at all. And yet purpose is what your customers want to see in your brand – they want to trade with businesses that are about more than money. They find them more trustworthy, more approachable and more enjoyable to interact with than sterile, product-led businesses. It's still possible to be a successful company without a purpose, but you'd have to have a good reason for not having one.

A human brand

Your brand is the ultimate way for you to express the humanity of your business. A brand is made up of so many elements: culture, story, history, artefacts, experiences, language, tone of voice, visual identity and purpose. Your customers experience it through various touch points, many of which are delivered by people, whether they be engineers on the road or customer care agents on the phone. In that sense, your brand is created for you through the quality of the interactions between these people and your customers, and through how they experience your product directly. Your brand isn't what you manufacture in the marketing department; it is – as Jeff Bezos once said – what your customers say about you when you're not in the room.

We all want to belong to something, to feel part of a tribe. In the same way, we want to belong to brands because they make us feel good and can impart a sense of purpose in our lives. We don't see them as random corporations to buy from but as experiences and values to buy into, of which the product is just one element. We want the human truth, and having a brand is the main thing that makes a business human.

Another way of looking at brand is as the ideal environment for your sales team. Just as plants can't flourish in a poor ecosystem, so sales can't grow without a brand that provides the nourishment they need. Marketing's job is to create a world in which, when sales people or lead generation campaigns swing into action, customers want to buy without being persuaded. To use another analogy, retailers understand the role of the shopping environment perfectly; we've all bought things in stores because we've been swayed by the ambience there: the design, the lighting, the music, the ads we've already seen. The context in which we buy something matters – it's part of the product itself.

What environment – conceptually, digitally and emotionally – are you creating for your customers so they're happy to pay a premium for your offering? Because one of the most valuable things a brand does is to allow you to command a higher price and to separate yourself from your competitors. Three companies can have the same kind of product, each charging more than the next. Apple commands twice as much as leading PC brands; Nike charges four times as much as non-branded trainers; Rolex prices itself multiple times higher than Timex. There may be some minor feature advantages in the pricier products, but nothing that would justify the price hikes on their own. It all comes down to how successfully the brands make their customers feel good about themselves.

This is no different – we repeat, no different – for B2B brands. If you recall Binet and Field's recommendation to invest 46% of your budget in brand building, with its emotion-led messaging, and 54% in lead generation, with its functional messaging, you can see how in the absence of a strong, human brand you're not maximizing your opportunity to grow. You're missing a vital component of the mix. Of course, we're not suggesting you should ditch lead generation activities or talking about product features entirely; we're just saying that B2B needs to re-balance. At the moment it's 95% features and lead generation, and 5% brand and emotion. It should be like the wings on a bird, with an equal balance between the two, because the way someone *feels* about your company is just as important as what they *think* about it. Unfortunately, B2B has lived on a product diet for so many years that it's going to take a revolution in thinking to enable it to take flight again.

This isn't easy because, let's face it, no one's going to stop you from carrying on as you are. You can continue to crunch the data to ascertain what your customers want; you don't have to make daring, creative leaps to imagine their desires instead. If you take the data route you won't have to go through the awkward process of trying to persuade your CEO that having a human brand to draw people to the company is a far more worthwhile investment than pulling yet another set of marketing levers. But the thing about the data is that it only helps you to pull the levers more cleverly; without the master brand lever to do the heavy lifting you'll always be running from one to the other, heaving them for all you're worth. It's not the most productive or enjoyable way to sell your products.

Human language

We human beings are simple creatures, and we yearn for B2B companies to talk to us in a more straightforward way. We don't want to be blindsided with facts and figures, jargon and tech speak – we really don't get turned on by this. And yet this is the approach most B2B marketers take. The technology and financial services sectors are especially guilty of this; sometimes it can be hard to understand what they're even trying to say. The people in these businesses seem to value coming across as professionals so much that they've forgotten how to talk in their customers' language; maybe they think they look clever, but they just look out of touch. And people are fed up with it, including (most likely) you. Have you ever played meeting room bingo or sighed when the latest update from your insurance company landed on your doormat? If you want to be a more human marketer, you need to mind your language.

Jargon always erodes trust, because there's no meeting in the middle between brand and buyer. They're on different wavelengths. If your brand's emails and social media updates are full of meaningless buzzwords and impenetrable language, you'll come across as yet another faceless company trying to sell things. It's so dry and dull, lacking in any kind of humanity or personality. Who would engage with that? Your company would be like that person no one wants to sit next to at a dinner party – more interested in spouting their own opinions than in engaging with their fellow diners.

This issue with language goes further than vocabulary; it also shows a lack of understanding of your customers' key pain points. Much 'business speak' consists of generic terms, such as 'solutions', that aren't specific enough about the problems they're trying to solve. Linguistic emotional intelligence is essential, because it's the evidence to your customer that you understand what they're going through. Anything that's written in an empathetic and human way has better cut-through than something that appears distant and irrelevant.

To see what we mean, let's look at a made-up example. You're the marketing director of an alternative finance company and your website says this: *We're the UK's leading alternative finance company. Our history in fintech goes back eight years, when we developed the first automated, end-to-end, peer-to-peer marketplace. Our loan approval system is the fastest in the market. If you're looking for a quick business loan, look no further.* This is what we call the language of product – so far, so standard.

Or the website could say this: *Last year we helped Frank and 400,000 other small business owners who lie awake at night, crippled by the thought of their business going bust. Without judgement, Jackie, one of our helpers, secured Frank a lifeline loan in under 48 hours. Frank's business is now back on its feet and he feels like a million dollars, although the amount we loaned him was significantly lower than this. All it took to stop the sleepless nights was a simple phone call to Jackie.* This is the language of emotion – far more impactful. It's writing to the human, not the machine. Buyers want to see themselves in the story you're telling them, which means you need to show that you understand them. If they can't see the direct relevance to themselves, your marketing serves no purpose; it's simply a story about you instead.

Having said this, a few B2B brands are differentiating themselves successfully through the language they use. Email platform Mailchimp is a good example, and is one of the go-to brands in its sector. Its platform and communications are less about the product and more about the brand personality. The chimp is a strong character, which makes the company memorable and appealing – a great example of a B2B brand taking on board the rules of good consumer marketing.

In case you're still feeling concerned about 'going human' with your language, bear in mind that it doesn't have to be simplistic or basic. You can still inject fun and personality into it, making your brand more likeable without coming across as dumb. The mistake many B2B marketers make is they would prefer to appear dry and distant than risk being direct and even a little playful, so they don't try new approaches. The end result is communications that look as if they've been designed by committee and that don't say anything worthwhile, as opposed to ones that stop people in their tracks and demand their attention. The latter is surely what you want.

The role of marketing

In its recent report 'The Modern Marketing Mandate',[1] IBM examines the role of the chief marketing officer

---

[1] IBM Institute for Business Value (2018). 'The Modern Marketing Mandate'. Global C-Suite Study, 19th edn. www.ibm.com/downloads/cas/W7D6L9EL

(CMO), as it exists today across both B2C and B2B. It notes how organizations are evolving from product-led business models to more human, experience-led ones: 'CMOs need to strategically address how to help their organisations compete by increasing value; creating exceptional, personalised customer experiences; and transforming corporate cultures to think and operate in truly customer-centric ways.'

This is no mean task, and in the ensuing struggle to adapt to these changes CMOs are falling into three broad archetypes, which IBM dubs the Reinventors, the Practitioners and the Aspirationals. The latter two groups can be summarized as those who are finding the transition difficult in various ways, but the Reinventors are the most interesting for our purposes here. IBM notes that experimentation is what the best CMOs do. This enables them to outperform the others in sales and profitability, as well as in innovation. They work in organizations which are well aligned, so their IT strategy is in sync with their business strategy, and their business processes support the overall strategic intentions. The companies they work for have a fluid approach and see constant change as a natural part of being a successful organization. Sadly, the report also points out that in B2B this doesn't really happen, or in such limited ways and with such low expectations that it has little impact on moving the business forward.

This touches on a key frustration for us, which is that while B2B has high ambitions of its growth targets, it has low ambitions of itself in terms of marketing. The two don't align. Other than at unusual times such as a recession and the recent COVID crisis, we don't suppose you've ever been to a board meeting in which an agreement is reached to hold back on growth projections for the year because everyone's a bit worried about how they're going to be achieved. When does that ever happen? And yet marketing is scared of shifting from an incremental approach to a transformational one. This is such a shame, because B2B is full of amazingly clever and talented people and if only they'd get on board with the idea of brand being the key to success, they'd fly.

Traditionally, the marketing team in B2B has always been the servant of sales. Sales drives everything, with marketing's role being to feed it leads, create bids and design brochures. Ironically, while marketing should be the one with the direct line to the customer, the only people who've always been close to customers have been sales people. And marketing has allowed this to happen. We've not heard of many CMOs who go out each week to spend time with customers, learning about their habits, issues and challenges, but sales people do. At the moment, the sales director and the CEO are in sync because sales brings in the numbers, but in a new future, marketing can be that deliverer of sales. It can be the CEO's best friend – the driver of growth. In this new world of data points and insights, marketing is smarter than it's ever been; if you use the technology and tools available to you, and get as close to your customers as possible, you can be the customer champion.

To be fair, there's an inherent complexity to B2B businesses as opposed to B2C. Sales cycles are protracted, products are complicated and many companies have evolved by acquiring other brands over the years, creating a confusing web of products and cultures that have to be communicated to customers. Add in a plethora of clever technologists and scientists, and multiple sales channels, and there's a hell of a lot to manage. In fact, some B2B marketers from a B2C background have found that their new environment has tested them like never before. If you're like many B2B marketers you've probably tried to cope with this by studying your products in depth; you don't want to be outshone by sales people and engineers who know more about the technical capabilities of them than you do. But stop: your intelligent naivety is your strength. It should be the person who *least* understands the product who does the marketing of it, because they're closer to the customer. And that's you. You'll want to make things simple and you'll question what engineers say. Marketing is the bridge between the product and its customers, and you're the keeper of it.

It's the way we're made

We human beings are pretty lazy. Our brains like to make quick decisions without having to process too much information, and this is as much the case with B2B customers as it is with B2C. Expending energy on understanding, and then communicating, the technical intricacies of your latest product upgrade is effort wasted; you'd be far better off taking a human approach and communicating the benefits instead. Customers won't rush to you because of your complicated, rational arguments, but because of your appeal to their emotions.

You'll learn a lot more about how our brains work in the next chapter, but for now we'd like to make one thing crystal clear: we human beings always buy on emotion and justify with facts. We rarely, if ever, go through a logical evaluation process and then decide what to buy, even if we think we do. In fact, Harvard professor Gerald

Zaltman claims that 95% of all purchase decisions are dictated by our subconscious mind.[2] Why? Because it's easier for us that way. When we decide to buy something, what's really driving the decision are our unconscious urges. There's plenty of research-based evidence for this, but as an example, take the fact that studies by neuroscientists have shown that people whose brains are damaged in the area that generates emotion are incapable of making any decisions at all. Humans are driven by feelings, which means that marketers need to sell the emotional benefits of buying a product, not the practical ones. Think of how B2C brands market themselves: luxury goods target our desire for self-worth, mobile phones for social connection and athletic brands for adventure and achievement. As Zaltman points out, it's the old marketing saying coming to life again: 'sell the sizzle, not the steak'.

Another way of thinking about this is to understand that our brains work in two different ways. In his influential book *Thinking, Fast and Slow*,[3] Daniel Kahneman summarizes the research he's undertaken over decades. His central point is that there's a dichotomy between two modes of human thought: 'System 1', which is fast, instinctive and emotional, and 'System 2', which is slower, more deliberative and more logical. Think of how much B2B marketing is done to the System 2 brain – the facts and figures, the speeds and feeds – and

[2] Chierotti, L. (2018). 'Harvard Professor Says 95% of Purchasing Decisions Are Subconscious', Inc., 26 March. www.inc.com/logan-chierotti/harvard-professor-says-95-of-purchasing-decisions-are-subconscious.html

[3] Kahneman, D. (2012). *Thinking, Fast and Slow*. Penguin.

how little to the more emotional System 1. Imagine for a moment what could happen to your sales if you switched your emphasis from machine to human; you'd be unlocking the 95% of purchase decisions that are there for the taking.

When was the last time you did something for the first time?

One of the most exciting things about moving to a human way of marketing is that it allows marketers to express their natural creativity. You may think your product is too dry to be creative with, but look at a company like Virgin Trains. Their ads are brilliant and stand out a mile from what other train franchises have done; they have humour, they're interesting and they're human. Creativity can make people want to get on the train or do things they've never done before. That's its power: to change a customer's perspective of your brand from this to that, so they take a leap.

Apart from anything else, creativity is the X-factor that differentiates you from the competition. How you use it in your business to represent yourselves is what makes you 'you'. It's the spark that separates Apple and Salesforce from their rivals, the trigger that makes you shell out for a designer bag instead of a basic one. The irony is that all B2B CMOs have access to the same resources as each other – the same marketing agencies, the same analysis tools. It's the way the visionary and creative ones mobilize those resources that makes the difference, because they've chosen to focus on human-centric and emotion-led marketing. They've replaced the product magnet with the brand one.

Creativity can also transform your career. In the IBM report we mentioned earlier, 'Reinventor' CMOs are identified as design-based thinkers who come up with new systems and ideas. They're designing their customer experiences in ways that capture people's imaginations; in doing so they're practising empathy and putting their customers' needs at the centre of their considerations. As the report says, 'Instead of focusing on how to market their widget or service, they ask, "What do our customers want? And how do we best serve their latent needs?"' Notice the word 'latent' here. These marketers aren't expecting their customers to tell them what they want; they're thinking laterally about how to meet their unconscious needs. This is where the true power of creativity and imagination comes in.

And yet B2B isn't changing, despite the fact that it makes so much sense for it to do so. We're willing to bet you spend a lot of time talking about change innovation in every other aspect of your business, from product development to technical transformation, so why not with marketing? Let's step off the treadmill and work out how to raise expectations of growth, challenge old product-centric assumptions and transform sales performance. Let's take B2B into the human world.

Key takeaways

o   B2B decision makers are people, just like you and me, and should be treated as such.
o   Customers, rather than products, need to be at the centre of your business.

o Having an overarching human purpose, and communicating it well, can make the difference between people buying from you or from someone else.

o Brand is the key element through which humanity and purpose are communicated.

o Marketing should be the function closest to the customer, not sales.

o It's creativity that makes the difference between incremental and transformational growth.

Part II

Humanizing B2B: What you need to know

The way we think

A good friend called me in a panic. He'd just left his doctor's surgery, where he'd been advised by his exasperated GP that if he didn't clean up his diet, stop smoking and start taking some exercise, he'd be at risk of ending his days in the ICU. My friend's response? To drive straight to KFC and comfort eat a bucket of chicken and fries.

We don't always take the logical course of action. In fact, we usually don't. We think, feel and do things that don't add up, don't stand the test of scrutiny and are impossible to justify in a rational way. Not only that, but much of the time we don't even realize we're being so illogical – it just feels like the right thing to do, so we do it. It's the same when we arrive at work; we don't suddenly turn into purely rational beings, making decisions on a functional basis alone. We don't turn off that part of us that makes us human – the quirky, emotional and instinctive bit. The aspect of someone we make friends with, fall in love with and feel loyalty towards. Can you imagine saying, 'I'd do anything for my colleague Peter, he's such a logical thinker – a really rational guy'? Of course not. You'd be far more likely to say, 'I'd do anything for Peter, he's good fun down the pub after work and never lets me down when there's a deadline to meet.'

So why, if we're fundamentally emotional beings, does B2B marketing spend all its time trying to appeal to the part of the brain that deals with facts and figures, logic and rigour? On the surface it might seem like a sensible thing to do – after all, you're working with intelligent buyers and sophisticated business people who need to give reasons for their decisions – but we've learned in recent years that this blind obsession with rational thinking is causing huge damage to the potential for business brands to drive growth and revenue. This, ironically, is a deeply irrational act in itself.

Here's another fact for you: people buy with emotion and justify with logic. This isn't our opinion; it's based on years of scientific research and it's 100% applicable to B2B marketing in the same way as it is to B2C. No exceptions. As we explored in the previous chapter, B2B has always known this in its own way, because not only did it incorporate emotional messaging in its marketing back in the day, but it also spent years investing in expensive sales people to build relationships with customers. Why else would it do that but for an innate understanding that feelings matter? Now the emotion has gone from our marketing and the sales people have dwindled too. And because marketing was left to cover off the rational bit with white papers, diagrams and return-on-investment projections, logic is all we're left with. It's no wonder that B2B marketing is known in some circles as 'boring to boring'.

So what is all this psychological science stuff? It's broadly split into neuroscience and behavioural science. Neuroscience is concerned with how our brains work, and here we'll be focusing our attention on the chemicals that are transmitted around our bodies and how they affect our thinking. Behavioural science is concerned with how we think, feel and act in certain situations, and what this means for our decision making. The two areas are obviously closely related and we expect you'll have heard of some of them already, but our aim is to show you why these findings are so relevant for B2B marketing.

We won't spend much time talking about reason because you're already a world expert in that; we'll assume you're taking it into account in your marketing. But we will explore why you should also be catering to both the irrational and instinctive aspects of human nature if you want to persuade people to buy from you. If you take what you learn in this chapter on board, you'll discover all sorts of exciting ways that marketing can be the true engine of growth in your business.

Personal chemistry

Neuroscience is the scientific study of the nervous system, which means it explains how we come to feel things in our bodies. Our brains have a process that's been there since our early ancestors evolved into humans that rewards us with happy chemicals when we take steps towards meeting our needs. It also warns us with unhappy chemicals when we perceive a threat or something that might stop us meeting those needs.[1] These hormones

---

[1] Breuning, L.G. (2016). 'You Have Power Over Your Brain Chemistry', *Psychology Today*, 20 October. www.psychologytoday.com/us/blog/your-neurochemical-self/201610/you-have-power-over-your-brain-chemistry

trigger feelings, and it's these feelings that we use as a navigation device to help us stay safe and well.

Notice that it's not *thoughts* that guide us, but *feelings*; we only know what we're thinking because we can feel it. If you don't believe us, try this experiment. If we were to ask you to summon feelings of anger right now, what would you do? Give it a go. (You can skip to the end of the chapter to see if we predicted correctly, and for the lesson you'll have learned.*)

In marketing, we're mostly concerned with the happy chemicals as they're the ones that persuade us to trust people, feel warm towards them and buy things from them. These hormones are dopamine, oxytocin, serotonin and endorphins. However, we'll also cover off cortisol, the main 'unhappy' hormone, as you also need to avoid triggering that with your marketing.

Dopamine

This is the 'feel-good' hormone that creates a rush of excitement when you anticipate a reward. In our hunter-gatherer days, dopamine would have given us a feeling of arousal when we came close to finding food, motivating us to carry on. Once we've experienced this surge we do more to trigger it again, which is why, in modern times, we keep checking our emails and social media feeds. That mild thrill we had when we first received a message from a friend is something we want to experience repeatedly. It can be addictive.

In marketing terms, think about how your messaging may or may not be encouraging your prospects to expect a reward. It might be through the tried-and-trusted route of special offers or limited-time discounts, but it might equally be through your customers feeling appreciated or recognized, and these emotions are far more enduring.

Oxytocin

This is a hormone secreted by the posterior lobe of the pituitary gland, a pea-sized structure at the base of our brains. It's often known as the 'cuddle' or 'bonding' hormone because it's released when we snuggle up with people we love, or interact with friends. It also causes us to bond with our own social groups; in one study, researchers found that Dutch students who were given a snort of the hormone became more positive about fictional Dutch characters, but were more negative about ones with Arab or German names.[2] This makes sense when we consider that in our ancestral times, leaving our social or family group could have meant serious danger. Oxytocin enables us to feel close enough to someone to trust them.

Studies have shown strong links between storytelling and the release of oxytocin; in fact, when people empathize with a story their oxytocin levels are on average 47% higher than normal.[3] This helps us to develop relationships with the characters in a story, even if they're not real. You can see how it's a hormone that's incredibly useful to marketers hoping to build bonds of trust between their

---

[2] Pappas, S. (2015). 'Oxytocin: Facts About the "Cuddle Hormone"', LiveScience, 4 June. www.livescience.com/42198-what-is-oxytocin. html

[3] Barraza, J.A. and Zak, P.J. (2009). 'Empathy toward Strangers Triggers Oxytocin Release and Subsequent Generosity', *Annals of the New York Academy of Sciences*, 1167: 182–189.

brands and potential customers, especially as people dosed with oxytocin are more willing to entrust their money to strangers.[4]

Serotonin

This chemical creates a calm feeling when we gain a social advantage, and makes us feel important. Because of our inherently social nature, we've evolved to assert ourselves to compete for natural resources; serotonin is released to reward us when we've 'won'. It's soon absorbed back into our bodies, meaning that we have to keep asserting ourselves again and again to feel confident. It therefore follows that remembering our past successes and focusing on happy times increases our serotonin levels. Even smiling artificially can give them a boost.

Interestingly, 90% of our serotonin lives in our gut, which is why we can have a 'gut feeling' about something. It's also why we often feel blue on a Monday, because overeating and drinking at the weekend has interfered with our serotonin balance. From a marketing perspective, think about how you can enable your customers to feel confident in relation to their peers so they associate that good feeling with you.

---

[4] Ellinger, N. (2016). 'Oxytocin and Direct Marketing: Beyond the Cuddle Chemical', Direct to Donor, 4 May. https://directtodonor.com/2016/05/04/oxytocin-and-direct-marketing-beyond-the-cuddle-chemical

Endorphins

If you feel high after a workout it's because of endorphins. They are the hormones that keep a long-distance runner going, and enable an exhausted or injured animal to run for its life. Humour and laughter also create endorphins, which is why we feel energized and 'high' when we share a joke with friends or watch a funny sitcom. At these times we're inclined to feel relaxed and spend money, so it's worth considering how you could use humour in your marketing.

Cortisol

This is our emergency hormone, triggered by pain or the anticipation of it. This pain can be comprised of physical threats such as hunger or injury, or internal threats such as social isolation or rejection. The release of cortisol creates an unpleasant feeling which motivates us to stop what we're doing and start focusing on something that will make us feel happier. It goes without saying that bombarding your customers with an overwhelming amount of details, facts and figures will cause them to avoid or ignore your marketing. The same goes for 'Act now! Save money! Don't miss this event!' If not communicated in the right way, this causes people to run a mile… in the opposite direction from your product.

The science of behaviour

Of course, we don't know what's going on in our brains and bodies with our hormones – they're released and transmitted without us being aware and there's little we can do to control them. What we do experience, however, is how we think and feel as a result of them being there. And our thinking is processed by two different systems in our brains.

In the previous chapter we referred to Daniel Kahneman's book *Thinking, Fast and Slow*, and his well-researched thesis that we have two modes of thought: System 1 (fast, instinctive and emotional) and System 2 (slower, more deliberate and more logical). System 1 is useful for responding quickly in a crisis, and enables us to complete routine or repetitive tasks without having to tax our brains unnecessarily, because it channels our thinking according to previous experience. It also leaps to conclusions, making heavy use of stereotypes and unconscious biases – in fact, it's a subconscious process in itself. System 2 enables us to reflect on the bigger picture, handle logic, solve problems and interpret data. It's harder work than System 1 and is a conscious, deliberate process.

In summary, these systems represent two different ways to form thoughts, each with its own characteristics. System 1 is associative, creating stories to explain events (with the disadvantage that it jumps to conclusions). System 2 is deliberative, analysing abstract concepts and tricky problems (with the disadvantage that it takes time and energy).[5] Try this conundrum to see what we mean. A bat and a ball cost £1.10 in total. The bat costs £1.00 more than the ball. How much does the ball cost? If you

---

5 'The 2 Ways the Brain Forms Thoughts', YouTube, 9 July 2015, user 'ConfidencePro.net'. www.youtube.com/watch?v=UxQvY1plvZA

answered £0.10, you'd be wrong; it's £0.05.[6] You'd also be in good company, because lots of people come to the wrong conclusion. But why is this seemingly simple maths question so difficult to get right? It's because we prefer to make the process of solving problems simple through the use of unconscious associations. In this case, most people substitute the 'more than' statement with an absolute statement, which makes the maths easier to work out.[7] Consider this next time you're tempted to pull together a ream of figures to convince your customers to buy – they'll draw their own conclusions based on their own unconscious associations, ignoring any logic you put their way.

Let's think about the implications these two systems have for the way we interpret things. Although we like to think our System 2 is in charge and knows what's going on (and that means all of us, even you), the truth is that System 1 primes our behaviour, even though we have no idea it's doing it. How many of each kind of animal did Moses take on the Ark? Of course the answer is 'none', because it was Noah not Moses, but so many people get this question wrong that it's been dubbed the 'Moses illusion'. Because Moses is also a biblical character, we associate him with the Ark – it's an example of what's known as priming. We use one element to make a chain

---

[6] If the ball costs £0.10 and the bat costs £1.00 more than the ball, then the bat would cost £1.10, to make a total of £1.20. The correct answer is that the ball costs £0.05 and the bat costs £1.05, to make a total of £1.10.

[7] Association for Psychological Science (2015). 'A New Twist on a Classical Puzzle', 11 May. www.psychologicalscience.org/publications/observer/obsonline/a-new-twist-on-a-classic-puzzle.html

of assumptions that lead to another, which may or may not be correct.

Priming is a form of cognitive bias. You've almost certainly learned about cognitive biases in relation to areas such as recruitment because they're mental shortcuts, or flaws in logical thinking, that lead us to irrational conclusions. But they also have huge implications for marketing. Let's take a look at the 12 main biases as analysed by Practical Psychology, and how they relate to our lives more generally.[8]

o Anchoring bias. We grab hold of the first piece of information we receive, no matter how unreliable it may be, such as when we negotiate a price based on the initial offer rather than coming at it afresh.
o Availability heuristic bias. We overestimate the importance of the information we have as opposed to what we don't have, such as when we worry about what we see on the news and ignore the everyday domestic dangers around us.
o Bandwagon bias. We believe something because everyone else does. Of course, no one thinks they do this, but they do. Think of when we sell shares because the stock market is falling, or change our minds in a meeting if everyone else thinks differently to us.
o Choice supportive bias. We defend our choices by noticing the advantages, rather than the disadvantages, of what we've gone for, such as when we justify

---

[8] '12 Cognitive Biases Explained – How to Think Better and More Logically Removing Bias', YouTube, 30 December 2016, user 'Practical Psychology'. https://youtu.be/wEwGBIr_RIw

spending money on a new car by talking about the fuel efficiency.

o Confirmation bias. We pay attention to information that confirms what we already think, such as when we listen positively to the political parties we support. This is one of the most widely used cognitive biases.

o Ostrich bias. We only consider the positive aspects of something and ignore the negative, such as when we procrastinate over changing bad habits or ignore health warnings on cigarette packets.

o Outcome bias. We judge a decision based on the end result, ignoring any other factors that were present at the time. For instance, we make a gut decision at work that turns out well so we assume all future decisions should be made this way; it may have been luck or some other element that caused the success.

o Overconfidence bias. We make decisions based on opinions rather than facts, such as when we splash out on a food item in premium packaging rather than checking the list of ingredients.

o Placebo bias. We believe something will have an effect, and therefore it does. The placebo effect is well known in medicine, with patients receiving sugar pills often reporting an improvement in symptoms.

o Survivorship bias. We judge something based on the surviving information. For instance, we assume that if certain successful business people have a similar approach to management, if we have it we'll be successful too.

o Selective perception bias. We perceive things based on our frame of reference, such as when we're looking to buy a new computer and suddenly start seeing ads for them.

o Blindspot bias. How biased are you? If we were to ask you, you'd say 'less than the average person'. We'll leave you with that thought.

We're a bit of a mess, aren't we? Well, yes – that's the point. We're far from rational creatures; in fact, we're constantly driven by urges way beyond our knowledge, let alone comprehension. There's a fascinating theory which Rory Sutherland, Vice Chairman of Ogilvy and all-round brilliant creative thinker, mentions in his book *Alchemy*[9] – that it's evolutionarily advantageous for humans not to use logic to inform their actions, but to use emotion instead. Rather, we employ logic to explain and defend our decisions to others, thereby elevating our position in the social group. As Sutherland puts it, 'In this model, reason is not… the brain's science and research and development function – it is the brain's legal and PR department.' It certainly explains confirmation bias and many of the other biases above. Self-serving arguments can work well if they're based on facts, but when it comes to the emotional and subjective world of buying decisions the situation is far more complex.

Which leads us to B2B marketing. Sutherland makes the point that it's especially important to understand System 1 thinking in advertising because when we're presented with something new we form an immediate and instinctive impression of it.[10] We use a gut reaction, and there's certainly no reasoning attached to it. System 2 is where the cogitation comes in, and as a marketer

---

[9] Sutherland, R. (2019). *Alchemy: The Surprising Power of Ideas that Don't Make Sense*. WH Allen, p. 123.
[10] 'Rory Sutherland on System 1 & System 2 Thinking', YouTube, 6 March 2016, user '42courses'. https://youtu.be/x5RKNJ7vI8A

you have to understand both; the worst thing you can do is to design a product or marketing campaign based entirely around System 2 and ignore System 1. Sutherland gives an example of a pension as being a classic System 2 product. It's logical to save for retirement and we know we should do it, but simply giving people a tax advantage to encourage them doesn't motivate System 1. What does work, however, is what the British government did a few years ago, which was to make signing up to a pension scheme the default action when starting a new job. This appeals to the 'lazy' System 1 thought process, which would rather avoid complex and tiring rational activities, plumping for the effort-free option instead.

Unfortunately, our propensity to deceive ourselves makes your job as a marketer quite difficult; no one wants to think they aren't aware of their own motivations, even if they accept this might be the case in theory. It therefore follows that even if you were to come up with a fabulously creative campaign that taps into your customers' unconscious desires, the likelihood is that your CEO will be happier to attribute it to the right data or a well-negotiated media spend than to your instinctive understanding of human psychology. Sutherland suggests that this is because we need a certain level of self-delusion to function as a social species. Imagine how difficult life would be if we had no capacity to deceive ourselves – we'd be forever feeling guilty or offending people. 'Would you like to go out with me? I'd love to learn more about your earning potential' doesn't really strike the right note. This is why research won't tell you what people's true motivations are, because they don't necessarily know themselves.

Instead of listening to what they say, you need to focus on how they feel and react.

The magical power of irrationality

We mentioned Rory Sutherland's excellent book *Alchemy* above, and the ideas in this section are drawn heavily from the thinking he reveals in it. The book is about the power of surprising ideas, and how what's missing in most marketing and product development (some B2C included) is the magic of the irrational. It turns out that we constantly do things that don't make sense and buy things when we 'shouldn't'. For instance, take the following product success stories that illustrate the weirdness of human nature:

o trousers made of a coarse, uncomfortable fabric that fades and takes ages to dry (jeans)
o a drink that consumers said they hated the taste of when it was first researched (Red Bull)
o a takeaway coffee that costs five times what it would to make at home (Starbucks)

And yet most B2B marketing is geared towards the binary, logical aspect of our brains – the bit that insists everything must add up. We need to understand the real triggers that cause people to buy things, rather than just the rational ones. And why don't we? Because we look at marketing through what Sutherland calls 'dodgy binoculars'. One lens is market research, which assumes that people have an understanding of why they do things and can therefore tell us (see the unconscious biases above for a debunk of that myth); the other is the standard economic lens which, while it has its strengths, is insufficient as a way of explaining human behaviour. As an example of the limitations of the economic lens, consider the fact that 68% of Americans would *pay* to have two weeks more holiday than the meagre fortnight they currently enjoy. Experience from other countries shows that this doesn't diminish productivity; in fact, it improves it. And yet in the logical model, productivity is proportional to the hours spent working, which means an increase in holiday allowance would reduce output. Economics doesn't always take human nature into account.

The economic lens leads you to do marketing which involves either bribing customers to buy something, or 'fining' them for not doing it. This is not only expensive but imaginatively limited. By having a deeper and broader way of thinking, you can not only come up with more creative ideas but also spot opportunities that might be game-changers – or even solve problems that have been stumping others for years.[11] Of course, your CEO and CFO hate experimenting with creative magic because of the uncertain outcomes; they prefer the incremental certainties that come with rational strategies, rather than those where the payoff is hard to calculate in advance but could be infinitely greater.

And yet it doesn't pay to be logical when everyone else is. Being rational is a simple mental process that's available to everyone, so you'll never stand out that way. It may be easy to defend and justify, but if you follow it on its own you'll only achieve the same results as everyone else in the long run. It can be hard

---

[11] 42Courses.com. 'Behavioural Economics with Rory Sutherland'. www.42courses.com/courses/behavioural-economics

to persuade the holders of the purse strings into this way of thinking but Luke Lang, co-founder and CMO at Crowdcube, suggests a nice way in. 'Modern B2B branding needs explaining in commercial rather than creative terms. You could say to the CFO, "Think of brand as your future cash flow", or, to a CEO, "Think of brand as the moat around your business that creates resilience when times are challenging."'

What this means for B2B marketing

It should be clear by now that your marketing needs to focus on how people feel, not on how they think (or rather, how they think they think). It's time to end this insane situation in which a knowledge of human physique is considered to be essential when designing a piece of furniture, but a knowledge of human psychology is not deemed important when designing a marketing campaign. B2B marketing has been getting it wrong for the past 30 years, because most B2B brands don't know how to tap into emotions and leverage their marketing in a human way.

This causes endless problems. As an example, during the COVID-19 pandemic we took part in a discussion panel about the subject of empathy in marketing as a way of achieving cut-through. As we talked, it became clear that so many B2B brands have only ever had a functional value proposition – one with commercial, rational messaging focusing on speeds and feeds. Not only was this turning off their customers in normal times, but it definitely wasn't landing in the current situation. Some of these businesses were starting to turn to more empathetic messaging, but without any pre-existing level of emotion they were finding it difficult to turn up the volume without appearing inauthentic. The brands that had invested in their emotional marketing, however, were able to forge a much more natural and organic sense of unity with their audience.

What do we mean by emotion-driven marketing? It turns out that there's a science to it that's well worth understanding.[12] Numerous research studies have shown that while we spend our lives swilling around in a huge range of human emotions, they boil down to four basic ones: happy, sad, afraid/surprised and angry/disgusted. They're as fundamental as the four ancient elements of the universe: earth, fire, wind and water – the things that make up everything we see, hear and touch. Let's look at each of these emotions in turn.

o Happiness. Our first emotional act in life is to respond to our mother's smile with one of our own. However, as well as being an enjoyable state, happiness is also a driver of action. It's the main instigator for social media sharing, for instance, because joy increases when it's spread around and we always want more of it. If your marketing makes your customers feel happy, they're more likely to buy from you.

o Sadness. When we're sad, we're more inclined than normal to understand and empathize with others. Studies have shown that when we feel this emotion we produce both cortisol and oxytocin; this is a powerful combination because it drives us to take actions that connect with and benefit others. In other words, it

[12] Seiter, C. (2014). 'The Science of Emotion in Marketing: How Our Brains Decide What to Share and Whom to Trust', Buffer, March 4. https://blog.bufferapp.com/science-of-emotion-in-marketing

makes us more generous and trusting, which explains why advertisers love using babies and children in advertising; they cause our brains to release oxytocin, thereby increasing trust and in turn sales.

o   Fear/surprise. This makes us desperate for something to cling on to so we feel safe. It can also cause us to feel a greater affiliation with a brand, the theory being that when we're scared we need to share the emotion with others (if no one else is around, a brand is a substitute). Fear can therefore stimulate people towards a greater brand attachment.

o   Anger/disgust. Anger can lead to aggression but it can also make us more stubborn; we've all experienced digging in our heels when someone's tried to persuade us out of a bad mood. It's not hard to see why anger and frustration aren't great emotions to stimulate in people you hope to buy from you, although many bank and insurance communications seem to ignore this fact.

It's clear from these four emotions that creating a sense of connection between brand and customer is essential. This is something you can't achieve with special offers or product feature comparisons. In an analysis of the IPA Databank, those with purely emotional content performed twice as well (31% as opposed to 16%) as those with only rational content, and also did a bit better than those whose content was mixed. This is because emotions are what have kept us safe for thousands of years; we're wired to pay attention to them rather than to logical reasoning, which has only been of use in the last few hundred years. So how can you achieve this balance?

This is something we'll explore more fully in the rest of the book, but for now you can consider the following.[13]

The first is to think about how you can present your product as being part of a larger movement. Apple does this extremely well; it recognizes that we're social creatures and want to be part of a revolution of sorts – one that elevates the importance of cutting-edge design and technology, and of creativity. Steve Jobs' famous product launch events made the participants feel important and special.

Another way is to use storytelling and narratives to engage your audience's unconscious emotions. As we mentioned earlier, stories stimulate oxytocin, which makes what you're saying memorable and relevant. They also create a phenomenon called neural coupling, in which the listener turns the story into their own ideas and experience. Reading or hearing a well-told story activates many areas of the brain, including the motor cortex, the sensory cortex and the frontal cortex, which is why it's such an involving experience – it takes you over and sticks around long after the telling is done.

A further way of creating a sense of connection is to find ways of generating trust. Companies that emphasize customer reviews and use human-centric case studies in their marketing are essentially saying, 'Trust us because others do'. This causes a gut reaction in their audiences, who are more inclined to buy from them due to the

[13] Smilovitz, S. (2020). 'Emotional Marketing Examples Scientifically Proven To Sway Buyers', Instapage, 10 November. https://instapage.com/blog/emotional-marketing

feeling of legitimacy that's been established; research shows that 70% of consumers read product reviews before purchasing, and that the reviews are 12 times more trusted than the company's own 'word for it'. But the reviews still need to be believable. Five-star reviews are not the most trusted because some people assume they're not genuine; four-star ones have the best credibility.[14] This is called the 'blemish frame'.

You could also consider the curiosity factor.[15] Your goal as a marketer is to gain people's attention, maintain it and connect it to your product. To do this, an element of intrigue and surprise can be extremely helpful because people love to join the dots between what they don't know and what they hope to find out – it's irresistible. Blendtec is a company making high-quality food blenders that it sells to both commercial and domestic customers. Its founder, Tom Dickson, is a charismatic and entertaining personality, who once had a habit of coming into work and seeing if he could use his products to blend all sorts of unlikely objects, such as golf balls and iPhones – with surprising success. Eventually the company created a YouTube channel called 'Will it Blend?' and now features videos on its website of him pulverising garden hoses, silly putty and hockey pucks, among other things. If you watch any

---

[14] Grothaus, M. (2018). 'Why Small Biz Owners Should Hope for 4-Star Reviews over 5 on Yelp and Google', Fast Company, 29 November. www.fastcompany.com/90273985/why-small-biz-owners-should-hope-for-4-star-reviews-over-5-on-yelp-and-google
[15] Martin, A. (2018). 'The Power of Content Chemistry: Release the Oxytocin!', EContent, 20 September. www.econtentmag.com/Articles/Column/Marketing-Master-Class/The-Power-of-Content-Chemistry-Release-the-Oxytocin!-127422.htm

of these we defy you not to feel curious about what a Rubik's Cube will look like when it's been turned to dust.

All these ways of developing a sense of connection with your audience are essential because it makes them feel like what they're experiencing isn't marketing, but a natural form of positive communication. We're all wired to make these connections – in fact, we're crying out for them. We need them to make our lives meaningful. It doesn't matter how advanced we become technologically – we'll always rely on our subconscious desires to make many of our decisions.

One of the points that Rory Sutherland eloquently makes in *Alchemy* is that the purpose of branded advertising in all its forms is to establish, in the minds of a company's audience, that it has a product that's been so heavily invested in that it would make no sense if it wasn't an extremely good one. He likens the interplay between brand and buyers to the symbiotic relationship between flowers and bees (both are organisms that have been around for millennia). While to a rational economist it may seem wasteful and inefficient for flowers to expend their energies on creating large and colourful petals, they do it to prove to bees that they're worth visiting for pollen. If a specific species of flower, with its distinctive plumage, were to repeatedly disappoint the bees, they would stop visiting it because they would recognize it as being different from the others. In this way, he explains, a flower is 'simply a weed with an advertising budget'.

What's more, the power of a brand can go further than simply signalling its intent through explicit marketing messages alone, such as 'buy from us because we're brilliant'. It can also build it into its business activities in an implicit way, a process we like to call developing a 'brand body language'.[16] Take, for example, the fact that Google has a unit in which entrepreneurs are coming up with ways of disrupting the company itself with whatever the next Google may be. This might seem like self-sabotage, but think about what it says about the business. It tells us that Google is more interested in birthing the next wave of innovative technology, and in serving its customers, than it is about protecting its own interests. That's powerful. It's these implicit communications that make up brand body language – the actions brands can take to prove their commitment to their core purpose, both to their customers and to society as a whole. They showcase the 'real' company – the stuff that happens behind the scenes.

The conclusion we can draw from this is that we're more inclined to value the meaning of things than the things themselves – to appreciate the way a product's marketing makes us feel, rather than whatever it is we're being asked to buy. It's no accident that companies that bring the magic of creativity into their marketing, such as Apple and Disney, are some of the most profitable brands around. Human behaviour is a messy, complicated and infinitely fascinating phenomenon, and the sooner you learn to dive into its rich depths and explore it, the more you'll increase your sales and build a legacy that will stand the test of time.

---

[16] Cash, P. (2020). 'Why Brand Body Language Matters', Rooster Punk Blog, 22 December. https://roosterpunk.com/why-brand-body-language-matters

Key takeaways

o Most of the time, we make decisions based on unconscious emotion and justify them with logic afterwards.

o Feelings are caused by hormones and chemicals travelling around our neural pathways; they drive our behaviour.

o We prefer to think quickly and instinctively rather than slowly and logically, because it's easier.

o B2B marketing needs to go with the grain of how human brains work and appeal to both emotion and logic, rather than to logic alone.

o It's only by embracing the power of the seemingly irrational side of human nature that B2B sales can achieve exponential growth.

* You thought of things that would make you angry, like the time your manager blamed you for something that wasn't your fault. You certainly didn't feel angry without doing any thinking first (or, if you did, you failed). It's the thought that creates the feeling, never the other way around.

The five principles of humanizing B2B

The beating heart of any business is its employees and customers, not its products. And as we've seen, customers aren't rational in their decision making – in fact, they're the opposite; they buy on emotion and justify with fact. It's this messy, illogical, human part of B2B that's the missing piece of the marketing puzzle, and to slot it into place you need to start turning your attention away from your products and towards your customers, colleagues and everyone else connected with your business. It's their fears, ambitions, desires and imaginations that should be the cornerstone of your marketing, not your product speeds and feeds. Of course, we're not saying that you should do away with all functional product explanations, just that they're not as important as you think they are.

The value of this lies in the fact that if you build a humanized brand you'll be creating an organization that's fit for the future, not only externally for your customers but also internally for your business culture. You'll have the opportunity to become the leader in your category, to exceed your revenue targets, and to show up in the market in a way that makes you far more than just a company that sells a product. You'll be creating an ethos in which the building of something amazing will turn you into a figurehead – someone who's doing something meaningful in B2B.

So how do you do that? In the years we've spent helping companies to humanize the way they market their products, we've come up with five timeless principles which we've found to be fundamental in shifting a brand from cold and technical to warm and appealing. Principles are basic truths, and putting these ones into practice will transform the way you do your marketing. They involve understanding that:

1. it's about people, not products

2. you need a purpose that's actioned

3. emotion is at your marketing core

4. likeability is transformational

5. storytelling is your vehicle

As you go through these principles you'll see that we've expanded upon some of them in the book already, and in fact you'll learn more about storytelling and likeability in the next two chapters. They're not rocket science, but they are brain science, and they're surprisingly easy to put into practice if you have a humanizing mindset. Once you understand them you'll start to challenge your thinking and strategize in a completely different way.

1 It's about people, not products

The first and most important principle is to switch from seeing products as being the most important part of your marketing and move your focus to people. When we talk about products, we mean not only physical items but also services and solutions – however you package up what you sell. And when we talk about people, we mean not only your customers but also your colleagues.

Let's start with your colleagues: your sales team, customer service staff, technical people, engineers and anyone else who comes into contact with your customers. These are the front line ambassadors of your business, which means that having the humanizing mindset shouldn't just be for the leadership team but for all employees. Everyone should feel like they have an important mission to take to the world when they interact with your customers.

The second aspect of people is, of course, your customers. Understanding their needs is the starting point of what makes you a human brand, so you have to be able to empathize and engage with them, not just sell features to them. In fact, the most significant change in B2B marketing over the last few years has been the shifting expectations of customers, and this is something that many companies have failed to keep up with. The things that customers want from you have changed beyond recognition; they demand a seamless service as the norm, and have a heightened expectation of what a brand should be. For many years now, all sorts of clever consumer brands have been busy building emotional connections and delivering outstanding experiential marketing, from shopping in an Apple store to buying with ease on Amazon. This has given B2B decision makers a new marketing baseline which they expect to be met in their business lives as well. It doesn't matter whether they're evaluating marketing software or buying a new outfit on Asos, they see themselves as consumers as much as customers or clients. Frankly, they're wondering why you're not exciting and educating them the same way as these consumer brands are doing.

Another change is that while the old world of B2B marketing was pretty macho and target-driven, we're now entering a more compassionate era. Brands that have embraced this are showing up well, recognizing that they don't always have to put out commercial messages in order to gain sales. We don't think B2B brands recognize how powerful gesture-based empathy can be when creating emotional connections with people – making them feel something, but also creating a commercial outcome, even if the return on investment comes further down the line.

An iconic story to illustrate this switch to people from products is what Pepsi did back in 1963.[1] At the time Pepsi was being outsold by Coke by a factor of almost six to one, and it wasn't the product that was the problem as much as the directionless nature of the brand. Coke had managed to convince the American public that it had bottled everything that was wholesome and good about American life. So what could Pepsi do about the situation? It brought on board a young advertising executive called Alan Pottasch, whose not inconsiderable challenge was to reinvigorate the Pepsi brand to compete with a functionally almost identical product that also happened to be the most successful of all time. To achieve this he made a game-changing decision, as he put it, to 'stop

[1] Nethercutt, Z. (2018). 'People Don't Buy Products, They Buy Better Versions of Themselves', Medium, 7 July. https://medium.com/s/buy-yourself/people-dont-buy-products-they-buy-better-versions-of-themselves-d481390bfcee

talking about the product and start talking about the user'. This was the first time a major brand had done this. Pepsi went on to create the idea of a new generation, one free from the consumerist messages being perpetrated by the mass media (remember, it was the 1960s) – a group of customers who would become known as 'The Pepsi Generation'. The marketing campaign for this simply re-imagined what people desired, which was to escape consumerism and by doing so (somewhat ironically) to buy a Pepsi. The people who bought into this were looking for a new way to think and feel, and Pepsi gave them that voice.

Pepsi's success with this not only enabled it to claw back a significant market share from Coke, but also inspired other brands not to sell *products* to consumers, but rather a better version of themselves. Think about how Apple does this. People don't buy its products because of what they do – there are others that function the same or better – but because of who they feel themselves to be when they use them. And there's no reason why B2B can't follow the same path, even 50 years after Pepsi led the way. This type of marketing is about feelings rather than features, and it connects with customers on a much deeper level than speeds and feeds could ever do.

Fundamental to understanding this shift in customer thinking is appreciating the difference between requirements, wants and needs, as experienced by your customers. Here's an example.

I require a new database because our current one is out of date. This is a **requirement**.

I require a new database because our current one is out of date, and I'd like to buy a new one. This is both a **requirement and a**

want. This person is in comparison shopping mode, and will choose a new product based on features.

I require a new database because our current one is out of date, and there's this one here that's amazing. I never knew databases could do this stuff – just think about the hours I could save and the beautiful reports I could run. I'll look amazing when I present to the board. This is a **requirement, a want and a need**. If you're the company selling this database, this customer is yours.

At the moment B2B is fulfilling its customers' requirements and even some of its wants as well, but it's not turning them into the emotional firestarters that turn them into needs – the ones they can feel as well as see. Examples of needs are the way that your product can solve your customers' underlying problems long-term, represent who they are as people by symbolizing their social status or personal identity (like Pepsi did), make your customers feel relaxed and rewarded when they use it or meet every expectation they have of it – both conscious and unconscious. Gallup research has shown that only 29% of B2B customers feel fully engaged with the businesses they buy from, and that 71% are at risk of leaving for a competitor. This is because their functional requirements are being met, but not their emotional needs. Engagement is a critical focus for you, because companies with the highest levels of it also have 72% more fully bought-in customers – a fact that should be giving you pause for thought when you think about where you place your marketing focus at the moment.[2]

---

[2] Viveiros, B.N. (2019). 'B2B Customer Experience: Why CX Matters across the Entire Funnel', Chief Marketer, 12 September. www.chiefmarketer.com/b2b-customer-experience-why-cx-matters-across-the-entire-funnel

Part of creating engagement is personalization. This is the concept of delivering pieces of one-to-one, or one-to-few, customized marketing content to your audiences, and it's an ultra-human way to go. Many businesses have invested in automated marketing platforms that allow them to market at scale, but this has led to a standardization of messaging which has been far from helpful in creating a sense of connection. Emails with personalized messages have higher open and click-through rates than non-personalized ones, and segmented campaigns result in significantly more revenue than non-segmented. To capitalize on this, in the last few years the notion of account-based marketing (ABM) has gained momentum. It's based on the idea that the closer you are to your customers and all the other stakeholders in their organizations, the more you're able to treat them as their own small marketing universe. This means that you can influence how your company is perceived, and therefore sell more of your products, than if you blast everyone with the same content. ITSMA's 2017 Benchmark Report showed that 87% of marketers say ABM leads to the largest increase in ROI over any other kind of marketing.[3]

ABM isn't only for your customers, but also for your prospects. Imagine you're the head of IT at a major software provider and your main focus for next year is to facilitate more remote working. You'd read blogs and online magazine articles on the subject to educate yourself, and consume content on the subject. If a

---

[3] Jackson, N. (2020). '10+ B2B Marketing Trends & Studies Every Marketer Should Know', Foundation Inc., 1 February. https://foundationinc.co/lab/b2b-marketing-trends

vendor with remote working solutions were to want to build a relationship with you and the other stakeholders in your organization, how would they be able to identify you and discover what you were interested in? They'd use a tool such as Cyance or 6Sense to access your intent-based data – the activity that tells them what you've been searching for. They could then ensure you're served adverts from their business which promote their remote working solutions in the very places you visit online.

An example of a company using ABM to increase sales is GE Healthcare.[4] It's moved to a highly targeted marketing strategy, and uses automation to track behaviours to sell lifesaving equipment to professionals in over 100 countries. The business delivers content to prospects 'upstream', recognizing that most of its customers make up their minds about a product way before they see a sales person. It also uses marketing automation to track what its prospect groups do online, using the information it gains to inform the content. It can even drill down to specific job roles, so marketers can tailor their messaging appropriately. This new personal touch has resulted in the company creating £1.3 billion in potential new revenue and £390 million in actual deals in its first year.

What we like about ABM is the positive influence it's having on B2B, in that it enables a deeper understanding of customers' needs and uses that has a way of building relationships. It doesn't, however, mean that it automatically creates emotional connections; you still need empathy and insight to do that, as well as the ability

---

[4] Chahal, M. (2015). 'GE Healthcare on how to Humanise B2B Marketing', *MarketingWeek*, 29 October. www.marketingweek. com/ge-healthcare-on-how-to-humanise-b2b-marketing

to generate human-oriented communications that spark conversations. But it does provide a way of humanizing B2B by enabling you to move closer to your customers, and to speak to them about their needs rather than just your products.

A note of warning here: being people-centric is not the same as being led by your customers, and nor should it be. Never simply trust in asking your customers what they want, because they don't know. For a start, what they think they desire isn't necessarily what they actually do (as we discovered in the previous chapter), but also, they can't possibly predict what you're capable of delivering given that technology moves on so quickly. None of us know what we want until we see it. It's your job to know what's possible and to lay out a vision that's so exciting that your customers can't wait to be a part of it. A great brand stands up for what it believes in, and by doing so becomes a magnet for people who believe in it too.

2 You need a purpose that's actioned

The most successful companies put an overarching purpose at the heart of their business. In fact, research by Deloitte states that purpose-oriented organizations report 30% higher levels of innovation and 40% higher levels of workforce retention than their competitors.[5] It also gives the example of Unilever, whose 28 'sustainable living' brands, such as Dove, Vaseline and Lipton, delivered 75% of the company's growth and grew 69%

---

[5] Deloitte (2021). '2021 Global Marketing Trends'. www2.deloitte. com/us/en/insights/topics/marketing-and-sales-operations/ global-marketing-trends.html

more quickly than the rest of its businesses in 2018. Soap, petroleum jelly and tea are everyday essentials, but a sense of purpose has given them a differentiation; the same can be said for B2B brands. What's more, an Edelman survey in 2019 showed that 61% of C-suite executives will pay a premium for a B2B service from a brand with a clear vision.[6] This makes finding your true sense of purpose a strategic imperative, but despite this the vast majority of B2B companies don't have one that's more than a statement on their boardroom wall.

Your purpose is the meaningful difference you want to see in the world – the reason why your company exists, above and beyond making a profit. When it's articulated and executed with authenticity and integrity, it becomes the wind in your company's sales. It's also closely related to people-centric marketing, because a purpose acts as a rallying cry for your colleagues and helps your market to see you for something more than what you sell. Microsoft, for instance, originally had the purpose of putting 'a PC on every desk in every home'. This is now 'empowering every person or organization on the planet' – a more human-centred aim that places its customers at the heart of what it does. Some businesses have a higher purpose such as solving a global problem, whereas others have one that's more focused on their specific sector or industry. You can have both, but there should be a clear link between the two.

However, purpose alone means nothing; it's the action you take and the commitment you show to your cause

---

[6] Edelman (2018). '2019 B2B Thought Leadership Imapct Survey', 5 December. www.edelman.com/research/2019-b2b-thought-leadership-impact-study

that defines your brand. This is the reason why our second principle is 'you need a purpose that's actioned' – it's to emphasize the implementation of purpose as much as the strategic side. It should become real for your customers at the various touch points they have with you, such as when they ring your call centre or meet your on-site engineers. Our experience is that many B2B companies know they need a sense of purpose, but the problem is that they don't have the knowledge and capability (or the will) to activate it. This is borne out by a new report called 'The B2B Purpose Paradox',[7] which shows that while 86% of B2B companies embrace purpose as being important to growth, they're yet to make it influence their business and social outcomes. What's more, only 24% say that purpose is embedded within their businesses to the point at which it can influence innovation, operations and their interaction with society as a whole.

Your starting point in making your purpose real is to develop an accompanying vision and mission, often called the purpose, mission, vision framework (PMV). Your purpose is what difference you want to make, your mission is the strategy you need to fulfil it and your vision answers the question of how the world will be different if you succeed. For example, one of our clients, Crowdcube, has this purpose: 'To fuel a new generation of businesses who want to leave a mark on the world'; their mission is 'To create an equity crowd funding experience that everybody loves'; and their vision is 'To create a world full of wonder brands fuelled by Crowdcube'. This is summed up in the storyline 'Funding the Wonderful'.

---

[7] Carol Cone On Purpose (2020). 'The B2B Purpose Paradox'. www.carolconeonpurpose.com/b2b-purpose-paradox

You can see how a mission and vision could change if necessary, but that your purpose should remain steadfast, and one of the wonderful outcomes of rethinking your business using the PMV framework is that you gain a clearer sense of your values and why they matter. It can be the catalyst for your leadership teams to reorient themselves around a more profitable and compassionate way of doing business, as well as to ensure that it's embedded throughout the culture. What's more, a strong PMV gives your marketing life and meaning, bringing your colleagues with you and – just as importantly – giving customers a reason to buy from you instead of from someone else.

There's such a lack of purpose in most B2B marketing that it's a refreshing change when a brand commits to being more than just a bunch of products. As Simon Sinek says, you know *what* you do, as do your customers. You may even know *how* you do it, in that you may have unique ways of delivering your product or service. But you almost certainly don't know *why* you do it (and it's not to make a profit – that's a result); your *why* is the thing that means no one else can touch you. In other words, 'Why do you get out of bed in the morning, and why should anyone care?'[8] We imagine you'd very much like for your colleagues and customers to care, and to buy from you because of it, not because you've got the latest feature that someone else will have copied by the end of the quarter. But for others to care, you have to care first, and having a purpose is the most powerful way of doing it.

---

[8] Sinek, S. (2009). 'How Great Leaders Inspire Action', TEDxPuget Sound. www.ted.com/talks/simon_sinek_how_great_leaders_inspire_ action

3 Emotion is at your marketing core

Did you know that, according to recent research by Gartner, the average decision making group in an enterprise-level, complex B2B purchase has increased from 5.4 people to 10.6 in the last 18 months?[9] It's not hard to see why this is; B2B buyers are human beings just like everyone else, and are more worried about making the wrong decision than they're excited by the idea of making the right one. Who can blame them? If you were to take a brave decision at work that bombed, you'd probably be facing a carpeting at your next review despite the fact that an unsuccessful but safe decision is rarely criticized in the same way. Here's where we have much in common with our friends in the animal kingdom; deer roam in herds, fish swim in shoals and even lions prowl in prides. It's security in numbers: 'It wasn't only me who made that decision, it was nine other people too. How could we all have been wrong?'

The way this plays out in B2B marketing is that, if you're trying to influence a complex sale and you know there are ten other people who will have a say in whether or not you win the contract, your chances of speaking directly with more than two or three of them are nil. The majority will either be too senior for you to access or be unknown to you. So how will they decide if they want to buy from you? What will form their opinion? We can tell you that it won't be one of your white papers or speeds-and-feeds downloads, it will be your website or what other people say about you. They'll receive a shortlist of options from the

[9] Gartner (n.d.). 'New B2B Buying Journey & its Implication for Sales'. www.gartner.com/en/sales-service/insights/b2b-buying-journey

front-line decision maker, head to relevant websites and check them out. If two are bland and factual, but the third one builds an emotional connection with them and gives them a sense of what the company's about, that will be the one they prefer. They'll use lazy brainpower, making snap decisions using their System 1 thinking even as they tell themselves they're being super rational and conscientious.

Our point here is that the way your brand shows up is crucially important on an emotional level because the more people who are involved in a purchase decision, the less control you have over the process. Your product has to speak for itself through your brand. The entire decision making team isn't going to wade through reams of factual information to make an informed decision; they rely on the three people you have direct contact with to do that. The result is that a two-year sales process can be won or lost on the impression that a c-suite executive has when he looks at your website for the first time. 'I don't like the look of those guys, there's something about them that doesn't feel right.' Or, 'Hmm, they look good. You know what? Let's give them a shot.' It can be as whimsical and as career-defining as that.

Although not all buying decisions are as complex as this, the fact is that whatever the number of people involved, your potential customers have access to more information than ever before. They have to sift through a mountain of seemingly high-quality data, work out how to prioritize what they need from it, and make sense of statistics from various different sources. Further research from Gartner has shown that they spend a full 15% of the buying cycle time reconciling and de-conflicting the information they have.[10] After all this stress and difficulty, it's little wonder that they're ready to plump for the company that speaks directly to their sense of ease, safety and comfort – in other words, the brand that makes them feel good.

Using emotion in your branding isn't just a case of finding a funny image or story and putting it on your website. It's about igniting emotion with everything you say and do. And it's about getting to know your audiences, using language and ideas that resonate with them, and finding ways to bring them into your story without them even realizing. Most importantly, it needs to be consistent, using what you know of your customers and your purpose to offer value in a human way. It's not about you or your products; it's about the people who buy them and the emotional connections you create.

This was the strategy we used when we helped peer-to-peer business lender Funding Circle to position itself as more than an afterthought for small business owners seeking loans. Because the traditional route for these traders would normally have been to approach their bank first and 'alternative lenders' last (meaning Funding Circle only got the borrowers rejected by the banks), the company needed to show it could be a viable first-choice solution. We knew we couldn't just describe the benefits of its offer – that would have been playing 'me too' to the banks. So we identified the *feeling* that small businesses wanted to have when they experienced any of Funding Circle's marketing activity. We realized that people brave

---

[10] Bryan, J. (2019). 'What Sales Should Know about B2B Buyers in 2019', Gartner, 1 February. www.gartner.com/smarterwithgartner/what-sales-should-know-about-b2b-buyers-in-2019/

enough to run their own ventures had a special love for what they did and a different outlook on their own potential. They weren't necessarily trying to change the world, but they did see it as important to follow their dreams and turn them into successful businesses.

We came up with the core storyline that these business owners were 'Made to Do More', as were those who invested in them through the platform. Funding Circle could bring them together, creating a feeling of belonging and recognition that would power them through the hard times and give them encouragement for the important work they do. We made this into a theme across all their marketing, turning the brand from a functional to an emotional one; the company even said it changed the way people behaved internally. The result was that it helped Funding Circle to double its growth and secure a £1.5 billion initial public offering (IPO).

4 Likeability is transformational

Have you ever worked for weeks on a pitch to a potential client, or painstakingly built a relationship with a prospect over months, only to lose out to another company for some reason that you never got to the bottom of? Have you ever built a new website to explain your product or service in glowing detail, complete with a comparison of features and benefits that your competitors offer (inferior, of course), only to see your sales go down and theirs go up? It's incredibly frustrating. What's going on?

It's the likeability factor. The reason you lost out is almost certainly because your potential customer just liked your competitors more. End of story. People want to do business with people they find amenable and trustworthy, even if their products aren't as good as the other person's. It's what the non-reachable executives in the buying group that we mentioned earlier did when they were asked to pick from a shortlist of suppliers – they chose the one they liked the most. As Rohit Bhargava says in his book *Likeonomics*, 'success has much less to do with *what* we create and much more to do with *who* believes in it'.[11]

We'll talk about likeability in much more detail later on, but for now we'll outline why it's so important as one of the five principles of humanizing B2B. For a start, there's a powerful link between being perceived as likeable and being seen as trustworthy, and, as we know, if you're going to spend a lot of money with a business and put your professional reputation on the line, a dollop of trust goes a long way. Have you ever trusted someone you didn't like?

In terms of execution, the important aspect of the likeability factor within the context of humanizing B2B is that it's important you *act* human. Robots are neither likeable nor trustworthy. Consider how you put your brand across in all your communications; what are you doing that's empathetic, honest and engaging? Because what you're trying to do with likeability is to create a bond or connection that will sway people's decision in your favour.

By the way, being likeable is nothing to do with being smarmy or superficial. People can tell the difference between genuine and false likeability pretty easily. The things your customers and prospects value in your

---

[11] Bhargava, R. (2012). *Likeonomics: The Unexpected Truth behind Earning Trust, Influencing Behaviour, and Inspiring Action*. John Wiley & Sons.

company are that it's happy to talk about what its other customers say about it; that it goes out of its way to be helpful without expecting anything in return; and that it expresses itself in a warm and personable way. Language, tone, personality, attitude, gestures and content all play into the mix of elements that make you likeable. It's time for you to jettison the 'professional' grey suits, jargon and purely intellectual content in your marketing – all it does is make you look the same as everyone else. You might come across as a safe pair of hands, but it's the most credible and likeable brand in your category that will win the business.

5 Storytelling is your vehicle

Storytelling isn't called a science for nothing. In fact, when we hear or read stories we automatically produce neurotransmitters that create different emotions within us. Presentations expert David Phillips gives a great TEDx talk in which he demonstrates how these chemicals help to suspend our critical thinking.[12] Being on the receiving end of a story releases dopamine, which improves focus, motivation and memory – all feelings you want to induce when you're selling to someone. Stories that are emotionally intense generate oxytocin, which increases generosity, trust and bonding – this allows your audience to feel a connection with your brand. And when you make people laugh with a story, even in a gentle way, this stimulates the production of endorphins, which encourage your prospects to feel creative, focused and relaxed. Phillips calls these three chemicals the 'angel's cocktail'.

---

[12] Phillips, D.J.P. (2017). 'The Magical Science of Storytelling', TEDx Stockholm, YouTube, 16 March, user 'TEDx Talks'. https://youtu.be/Nj-hdQMa3uA

There is also, however, the 'devil's cocktail' to consider, which is a mixture of cortisol and adrenaline. These cause people to become intolerant, critical, forgetful and to make bad decisions – not a drink you want your audience to be consuming when they're engaging with your marketing. And yet, which state of mind do you think is produced by graphs, charts and data sheets with complicated explanations of product features? And which is encouraged by the telling of an engaging, interesting and emotionally charged story? The fact is that when we tell stories we're not marketing to people, we're marketing to chemistry.

Your customers are increasingly interested in the human beings behind the public persona of your business, and they'd love to hear compelling stories about them or those you have an effect on through your work. This kind of approach helps them to feel less as if they're being sold to and more as if they're being treated like family. No one wants to think they're the target of a sales pitch, but they always enjoy a good story. After all, when you recommend a product or service to a friend you don't rattle off a list of features, you share how it had an impact on your life – you're telling a story without realizing it.[13]

Storytelling is also an excellent way to show empathy with your audience. Who doesn't want to feel deeply understood? There are actually three levels of empathy,

---

[13] Hyder, S. (2018). 'How to Humanize B2B Marketing to Accelerate Growth', *Forbes*, 7 December. www.forbes.com/sites/shamahyder/2018/12/07/how-to-humanize-b2b-marketing-to-accelerate-growth/#69709a0a6146

as explained by psychologists Daniel Goleman and Paul Ekman.[14]

o Cognitive empathy – the ability to understand the thoughts and feelings of others. This makes you a good communicator because it enables you to impart information in a way that works for them.

o Emotional empathy – the ability to share the feelings of others. This helps you to build emotional connections because you understand *why* they feel the way they do.

o Compassionate empathy – this goes one step further and moves you to *take action* to help others. When linked into your company purpose, you can imagine the power this has in your communications.

When you develop a connection with your audience through empathy, and when you tell stories that have your customers at the heart of them, you're concocting a magical combination that automatically makes you a human marketer. Storytelling is a fantastic way of reminding yourself that there's a human being at the other end of your marketing, and it's something you'll learn a lot more about over the page.

We created these five principles to show you that humanized B2B marketing is not as complicated as it might seem; in fact, you're probably doing some of them already. Putting people instead of products at the heart of

---

[14] Bariso, J. (2018). 'There Are Actually 3 Types of Empathy. Here's How They Differ – and How You Can Develop Them All'. Inc., 19 September. www.inc.com/justin-bariso/there-are-actually-3-types-of-empathy-heres-how-they-differ-and-how-you-can-develop-them-all.html

your marketing, creating an actionable purpose, treating emotion with the respect it deserves, becoming a likeable brand and learning how to tell great business stories – these are the cornerstone activities of making your company human. There's nothing weird or wonderful about the principles, just common-sense thinking about what draws customers to your company.

Key takeaways

o The five principles of humanizing B2B are the simple strategies for transforming your sales.

o Focusing on people rather than products turns your business into a problem solver rather than a sales pusher.

o Having a purpose gives people a unique reason to buy from you, and to be loyal as well.

o Giving the power of emotion the status it deserves in your marketing creates deep connections and engagement with your audience.

o Being likeable generates the all-important level of trust that buyers need before they engage with you.

o Storytelling is how you turn your product into something memorable and meaningful.

Storynomics

Creating a culture of storytelling in B2B marketing is a bit like the endless quest for self-improvement. Everyone knows they should be doing it, but somehow it never happens. As with any new endeavour, it helps to know why you're doing it first, because if you have a nagging doubt as to whether it really would transform your sales you'll forever sit on the fence, waiting for someone else to try it first. By which time, of course, much of your advantage is lost. If only there was some concrete evidence to prove its worth...

Thankfully, there is. In 2009, two guys called Rob Walker and Joshua Glenn came up with the idea of buying 100 cheap trinkets from thrift stores and asking a different professional writer to invent a story about each one.[1] The stories were intriguing, inventive and fun; for instance, a heart-shaped paperweight was accompanied by a tongue-in-cheek tale about an office manager who used it to weigh down the lid of her jar of M&Ms. Walker and Glenn then listed the items on eBay together with their stories, to see if the

[1] You can see all the items and their stories here: http:// significantobjects.com

value of the objects was enhanced. The results were staggering. From an original outlay of $129, their sales totalled nearly $3,600 – a profit of over 2,700%. This experiment, dubbed the 'significant objects project', demonstrates the power of stories and the emotional value they add, to the extent that they can transform insignificant objects into significant ones. The people who bought the items were willing to pay more simply because they had a story attached to them.

Let's look at how this translates into B2B marketing. The standard way to increase your prices and profitability is to add new features and charge more for them, even if your customers don't really need or want them. This is lazy thinking. Now you can see there's a better way, which is to focus on the story you tell instead. If you sell a software subscription service for £17.99 a month, having a credible and compelling story to go with it could transform its worth to £25 in your customers' eyes. Not only that, but the value you've given it, and the space you subsequently occupy in people's minds, would help to differentiate your product from your competition. Not only is your offering more worthwhile to them, but you're also more noticeable in the first place. This is the economic advantage that storytelling can bestow upon your business. You could call it 'storynomics'.

It goes further than this. Storytelling is at the very heart of humanizing B2B. It's not just about spinning a tale to make a product more interesting; it's part of the essence of what makes your business more appealing than someone else's. It's interesting that when Steve Jobs returned to Apple after his stint at animated film studio Pixar, he brought back the storytelling skills he'd learned there to the development and promotion of the iPod, iPhone and iPad – products that transformed Apple's fortunes.

That's why it's so critical to understand what makes stories so powerful and to learn how to create your own. In this chapter you'll discover what makes stories such a force to be reckoned with in B2B marketing, the ingredients you need for them, the basics of constructing a story, what makes a story that works and the basic principles of storytelling. Along the way, you'll see examples of stories that have transformed the fortunes of the companies that have created them.

Why stories work

We've talked about why storytelling should be an essential part of your B2B marketing at various points in this book, but here we're bringing together our thinking and expanding upon it. The truth is that there are a number of reasons why stories work so well.

They make your facts memorable

Think about the last film you saw or novel you read. What happened to the main character? Where was it set? What did you feel at the end? You can probably bring to mind all these things, but we doubt if you can do the same for the last data sheet you came across. You might recall the odd statistic, but you'd be hard-pressed to give a fluent description of the content. That's because stories make facts memorable – 22 times more so, as research shows. Sally Croft, VP of Marketing, Communications, Government Relations and CSR at Ericsson, makes the point that in marketing we have a huge amount of data but little ability to craft a story from it. Stories turn facts into 'actionable intelligence'.

A narrative structure is an excellent way of giving your brain 'hooks' to hang the material on. This is why 'Our software will cut your service costs by 30%', while impressive as a statistic, is not nearly as memorable as a story about Joe the operations director who came back to work after sick leave, only to be tasked with slashing his department's costs within the next three months. His team, aware of the cost-cutting rumours, was demoralized and stress levels were high. He didn't know what to do, but when he discovered the new software and switched to it he was able to achieve the required savings without making any redundancies. He was also given a substantial bonus for his efforts and became a hero to his colleagues. The next time you make a sales presentation, how about putting your entire PowerPoint onto five slides as a story like this?

They give your audience reasons to care

As the writer Maya Angelou once said, 'I've learned that people will forget what you said, people will forget what you did, but people will never forget how you made them feel.' Given that storytelling is the language of emotion, it's the perfect vehicle for your messages. When you tell a great story you set up excitement and suspense, stimulating all sorts of emotions in your audience that make them feel personally involved. In other words, being on the receiving end of a story is an emotional investment which your audience is willing to make if it's entertaining and compelling enough – they're swept along.

As we've discussed previously, these feelings are caused by chemicals called neurotransmitters that are released when we're exposed to different elements of a story. Plot devices containing suspense stimulate the release of dopamine, the 'reward' hormone, which improves our focus, motivation and memory. Stories which encourage us to feel empathy towards the main character, such as we might feel towards the hard-pressed operations director above, cause the 'cuddle' hormone oxytocin to flow around our bodies. This increases the level of trust we feel towards both the storyteller and the story. And when a narrative is even a little funny and touching, we produce endorphins, which make us feel focused and relaxed, much like after you've been for a run or had a fun night out with friends.

Focus, motivation, trust and relaxation – are these the states of mind you would like your customers to be in when they read your marketing materials? We think so. And are they the ones they're likely to be in when you present them with a dull ebook or features comparison chart? We think not. It's not that they don't need the facts and specifics, it's that data alone isn't enough. Numbers and facts wake up our inner critic, switching on the part of our brain that analyses and finds fault with things. Stories, on the other hand, lull us into a receptive and trusting frame of mind. Or, as Michael Margolis says in his book *Story 10x*, '... meaning doesn't come from numbers. Meaning comes from the story about what these numbers represent or tell us.'[2]

---

[2] Margolis, M. (2019). *Story 10x: Turn the Impossible into the Inevitable*. Storied, p. 7.

You might think you'd never be 'hoodwinked' by a story, but it's important to acknowledge how subconscious the emotion-based decision making process is. Because feelings have evolved in order to ensure our survival, they're too important to be left to chance, so our bodies produce them without us making a deliberate decision about it. Which means that stories that produce emotions conducive to buying will always lead people to your door, whether they intend to make their way there or not.

They make sense to us in a way that nothing else can

The journalist and novelist Will Storr makes a critical point: what storytellers say about how to tell stories is the same as what psychologists say about how we live our everyday lives.[3] In other words, 'story is what brain does', to the extent that we experience our lives as if we're the hero of our own story – overcoming challenges on a daily basis and turning into a different person at the end.

As Storr puts it, all stories are based on change, and change is what our brains are hard-wired to pay attention to. It's an inherited part of our survival instinct; scan a clear horizon and we're safe, but see something moving across it and we're in possible danger. From earliest times, we've used stories as a way of educating our fellow humans about what to do and not to do; follow that trail and find healthy berries, or follow the other one and find poisonous ones. At the same time, stories (or, more accurately, gossip) have always been powerful instruments

---

[3] Storr, W. (2018). 'The Science of Storytelling', TEDxManchester, YouTube, 20 March, user 'TEDx Talks'. https://youtu.be/P2CVIGuRg4E

for creating bonds within groups, with the villains who destroy the harmony of the tribe being punished and the selfless people who work for the good of others being accepted and therefore safe. This is why, at the beginning of any great story, something surprising and unfair tends to happen to the main character. We want to see how they deal with it, and are led on a journey of challenges and changes which ultimately result in a restoration of order and an enhancement of the character's inner capabilities. This is the ambition we have for our own lives.

Stories also play to our innate desire to be in control, because we like to see ourself as the instigator of action, not as the passive recipient of it. Or, as Miri Rodriguez, creative journalist at Microsoft and author of *Brand Storytelling* puts it, 'customers want to win, they don't want to be sold to'.[4] Through listening to a story, we have the chance to step into the main character's shoes and grow with them, which appeals to our desire to be the main influencer over our lives. And to experience that sense of control, we need to know what happens next. Will the hero solve their dilemma? Will they receive their just reward? And how will they feel at the end of it? When we absorb a story what we're really doing is asking ourselves, 'How do I control the world? What do I have to do and be?' And by the end of it, if it's a good one, we'll find the answer. Think about your own life. We bet you face various problems all the time, and your primary desire is to wrestle them to the ground and control them. Stories

---

[4] 'Brand Empathy and the Next Wave of Storytelling: Episode 01', YouTube, 13 April 2020, user 'Geometry'. https://youtu.be/7VQQIo7Jnp0

are one of the most effective ways we have of giving us authority over our fears.

You can see from this that consuming stories reinforces our instinctive beliefs and assumptions about life and makes us feel better about them. This is pretty deep stuff, and what it means for you as a B2B marketer is that you're going with the grain of human nature when you tell a story. If you can find a way to talk about your business and products in the context of a narrative, you're effectively inserting your message into the willing brains of your audience. The alternative is to desperately jump up and down, waving a white paper or data sheet.

They build your brand

To many CEOs, the word 'brand' means logos and visual identity, or the 'colouring-in squad', rather than the powerful force that can transform their sales. However, many do understand the need for storytelling in their businesses. This is why, when we talk to new clients, we often use storytelling as a proxy for brand building. When we say, 'If you had a better story to tell, do you think you'd sell more products and encourage your employees to feel more engaged and productive?', the answer is 'Yes'. We could just as easily be talking about brand, but we find that storytelling is our Trojan horse to address the subject.

The ability of stories to build brands is fundamental to their power, as some interesting research shows. The agency network Havas set up a division some years ago to analyse brands, and every two years it undertakes a global survey of consumers to identify which brands are most meaningful in their lives.[5] From the most recent survey in 2019 the resulting brand index shows that, sadly, people wouldn't care if 77% of the world's brands disappeared tomorrow. This is terrible (although not surprising to us).

Why are these brands not valued? It's because people don't feel emotionally connected to them. Ones that do make the cut, such as Samsung and Google, have created meaning for themselves. Our point here is that storytelling generates emotional value and brand worth. With the previous 2017 Havas survey showing that the most meaningful brands outperformed the stock market by 206% in the last ten years, this is worth taking note of.[6]

Storytelling isn't just another fad or even another lever in your marketing machine. In fact, it's the oil in the machine that makes everything work better. By incorporating it into your presentations, videos, website, events, experiences, social media and other marketing levers, each of their effects will be amplified. For instance, you can carry out much better ABM and content marketing if you look at them through the lens of storytelling. This is because of how hardwired we are to listen to stories; as social psychologist Jonathan Haidt has said, 'The human mind is a story processor, not a logic processor.' Your customers are desperate to buy from companies they trust, so why aren't you using the number-one vehicle for generating trust – the oxytocin-producing story – to transform your brand?

---

[5] See: www.meaningful-brands.com/en

[6] Havas (n.d.). 'Meaningful Brands', powered by Havas. www. meaningful-brands.com/en

Story structure and planning

We hope you've bought into the need for storytelling in B2B and are keen to learn how to create your own stories. But before we dive in we need to clear up a common misunderstanding, which is that a story isn't always a story – even if it seems like one.

Take this example: 'We're the world's leading provider of mission-critical digital transformation services to global enterprise companies. Our hybrid cloud approach provides flexibility and security for extra peace of mind. Our skilled consultants use a combination of people and machine learning to get digital projects back in line with organizational goals. We call our approach intelligent design transformation, or IDT for short. As a Fortune 500 company, we're trusted by 42 of the world's top 50 companies. Visit our website for more information.'

Apart from 'Ugh', what did you feel when you read that? Pretty much nothing, because a bunch of words can't make up a story if it doesn't connect with people on an emotional level. It's not a story if the company jogs up with techno-babble and geek speak, or if the central character is the brand, not the customer, or if people don't understand it after they've read it. It's also not a story if the company's customers don't see themselves reflected in it. It's simply a business descriptor.

This is a story.

Running a global business in an uncertain world is a struggle for even the smartest CEO [see how we've name-checked the target audience and created some context]. *Never-ending digital transformation projects can suck up resources and stifle the growth they're intended to create* [we've added conflict and empathy]. *At Newco1234, we've made it our mission to solve this problem. We simply help the world's smartest CEOs* [they're the heroes, with the brand as the enabler] *to stay one step ahead by getting their digital transformation projects back on track. We call what we do 'Running Smart'. Find out why, when their reputation is on the line* [we've shown them what's at stake], *42 of the world's top 50 CEOs run smarter with Newco1234* [we've introduced a storyline about running smart. What CEO doesn't want to run smart?]. *Find out how to run smart at www.newco1234.com.*

In this we've made the customer the hero, highlighted a problem, positioned the brand as the enabler and created the idea of 'running smart'. We've also talked about something that's important, which is the reputation of the CEO – this brings emotion into the story.

Let's explore the structures of compelling stories. Because storytelling is often used as a generic word to describe different types of marketing activity, we've found it helpful to break it down into three levels, each with its own purpose, strategy and tactics. There can be some confusion about storytelling in B2B in terms of how it can work on a practical basis, and these three levels help to clarify things.

Level-one storytelling: Organizational

Like every business, yours has many stories to tell, but the most important story, the one that creates real clarity, is the organizing story. This story is transformational, inspiring, game-changing and category-defining. It shapes your vision, enhances your company purpose, inspires your customers and rallies your teams. It also creates awareness and desire for what you do, moves markets and – most importantly – inspires people to see the world like you do. Other level-one stories exist around your company's origin and heritage, social responsibility, sustainability, customer service, culture and innovation. These stories are essential for creating a high level of emotional engagement with your customers, employees, communities and within wider society. You can put them to work through effective brand positioning, thought-leadership, change management and employer branding.

Level-two storytelling: In-market

All businesses need to drive demand for their products and services. Often in B2B-Land it's easy to be distracted by features and benefits which result in 'me too' campaigns that do little to excite or entice customers. Level-two storytelling is about taking a more creative and story-first approach to improving the results you get from traditional ABM, marketing campaigns and lead generation activities, all with a clear focus: driving engagement and sales. It enables you to create a meaningful connection with people on an emotional (not product) level, to drive effective customer acquisition and retention. The purpose of level-two storytelling is to move your prospects through your sales process, and to reassure and engage your existing customers. Stories at this level are used in sales campaigns, product launches and all types of customer-driven events.

Level-three storytelling: Tactical

These stories are tactical and in-the-moment, taking existing marketing content and presenting it in an engaging and interesting way. The vehicle could be a PowerPoint presentation at an internal event, a product animation at a user conference or simply a more engaging way of creating customer case studies. You can see level-three stories being executed when there's a need to explain the results of an initiative, or to sell a specific aspect of what a business does in a way that's more compelling than basic facts and figures.

One of the most interesting developments we're seeing is the need to combine level-one and level-two stories so they're connected. At the moment brand and lead generation activities each sit in their own silos, but by bringing together organizational and in-market stories marketers are able to leverage the power of brand more effectively. We like to call this 'brand generation' (brandgen) as it combines branding and lead generation into one.

Having said that, level-one storytelling is where brands should start. This is where your company's purpose, mission and vision sit – the elements that bring together hearts and minds. The second level is more functional, supporting the needs of the business and driving sales, and the third level is basic security. In our experience, less than 5% of B2B brands have a level-one story, which is incredibly exciting for us – and should be for you too – because it means there's a transformative opportunity out there just waiting for you to grasp it; 95% of the world's B2B companies can still benefit from having a story at the heart of their business – how about that?

Let's explore the power of the level-one story, linking it to the simplicity of Simon Sinek's 'Start With Why' concentric circles.[7] Most companies start from the outside circle and talk a lot about *what* they do (level-three storytelling), while some may talk about *how* they do it (level-two storytelling). But very few explain *why* they do it. Level-one storytelling is your purpose – your *why*.

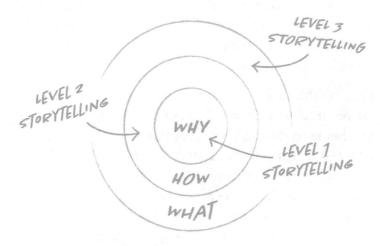

The golden circle
© Rooster Punk 2021

Just as the most profitable and successful businesses start from the inner circle with their purpose, so it follows that the best companies do the same with their storytelling. Of course, to do this they have to have an actionable purpose in the first place, which is one of our five principles of humanizing B2B. Even when we talk to companies that have taken the time to articulate their purpose, we find they

---

[7] Sinek, S. (2009). 'How Great Leaders Inspire Action', TEDxPuget Sound. www.ted.com/talks/simon_sinek_how_great_leaders_inspire_action

often see it in isolation rather than packaging it up in a story. Your purpose, mission and vision are the raw ingredients of your organizing (level-one) story, and they need making sense of for your audience through storytelling.

What you really need is a blend of all three levels that's unique to you, because it's the cumulative effect of the different types of story being told over time that creates your brand presence. The more unity there is in the stories you're telling, the better. If you tell them from the bottom level up you'll always be trying to find new stories to create, whereas if you start from the top, everything else will feed into your organizing story. As Darryl Bowman, CMO at Receipt Bank, puts it, 'Find a story and say it in everything you do. Reiterate and repeat all the time. Even if you get bored internally, it often feels new to your customers.' This is, after all, what creates credibility and consistency in the minds of your buyers.

Models and tools for great storytelling

You've probably heard of the notion of a story arc, and how all stories follow the same basic pattern. Although there's much truth in this, the reality is that although there are various formulae for telling a good story, they're only guidelines. And there's no one right way to do it – there are thousands of permutations in the way you can combine your storytelling ingredients. The most important thing is that your story is a reflection of your brand. And while you can (and should) read countless books on storytelling techniques, your primary aim is to gather your audience around you and to share your unique adventure with them in a way that informs, inspires and entertains. That's what a good story is.

Archetypes

The psychologist Carl Jung created a number of archetypes, 12 in total, which he defined as universal, archaic symbols that derive from the collective unconscious. We've studied these archetypes and have brought them into the B2B story context, creating four higher states that people can identify with as customers. They are:

o belonging
o legacy
o structure
o independence

These are the four states we want from our interactions with brands. We're either seeking a sense of belonging, a desire to leave a legacy, the reassurance of structure or the excitement of independence. These states aren't mutually exclusive, so it's possible for a brand story to be about legacy but also belonging. And you can have one dominant story accompanied by a secondary one. These states and archetypes are useful when you're thinking about how your brand can resonate in the lives of your customers. Crowdfunding company Crowdcube, for example, is focused on the states of legacy and belonging, with the brand building a strong sense of community for entrepreneurs. Whichever supporting archetype you choose, you'll be allying yourself with what Miri Rodriguez calls a 'universal truth', which we can all attest to, because it generates the same feeling in us all.[8]

---

[8] 'Brand Empathy and the Next Wave of Storytelling: Episode 01', YouTube, 13 April 2020, user 'Geometry'. https://youtu.be/7VQQIo7Jnp0

Brand archetypes model
© Rooster Punk 2021

Once you've identified your purpose, your next task is to decide which archetype you could use to position your brand within that state. The archetypes help you look at your brand and story with the added benefit of personality, attitude and beliefs. For instance, if you sell a software package that tracks all the mobile phones a company owns so that purchasing managers can control them, does your product bring structure and order to that manager's life? If so, your story might run along the following lines.

It's a headache keeping track of all those handsets and contracts. You feel stressed and out of control. Our software helps you manage them all in one place instead, so you can sleep at night without worrying.

Or does it create a sense of belonging?

You feel isolated as an IT buyer with all the phones you have to manage. We help 75% of companies like yours to keep track of them all. If you come to us, you'll have the security of knowing you're part of a community in which you can share advice and ask for help from other buyers.

You can see how the same product can work with different story archetypes.

The key element in creating a brand story is that, 90% of the time, your customer should be the hero. The mistake a lot of companies make is to allocate that role to the brand or product, but you need to remember that your buyer wants to see themselves cast in the central starring role, recognizing themselves in the story. Your brand is the enabler for their success, not the other way around. For instance, if your customer is the purchasing manager above, they should be saying to themselves, *'I'm just like that person – I have the same kind of problems, and look how this brand is helping them to solve them and boosting their career at the same time. I want to be like that manager.'*

By putting themselves in your hero's shoes, your customer is empathizing with your character and buying into the story.

So what should this hero be doing in your story? Here's where what have become known as the seven key plot outlines come in. Note that these aren't the same as the archetypes above, which are centred on states of mind.

These are narrative structures that give you hooks to hang your story on. You'll recognize many of them, and your job is to decide which plot will best suit your overarching purpose, allowing you to put your customer at the heart of your story and present your brand's meaning and value in the optimum way.

o Overcoming the monster (*War of the Worlds*). The hero overcomes enormous challenges to defeat his opponent.

o Rags to riches (*Cinderella*). An underdog rises above their station in life as a result of their own efforts, to defeat the villain.

o The quest (*Star Wars*). The hero goes on an epic journey, often accompanied by allies, and rises to challenges with the aim of recovering something that has been lost.

o Voyage and return (*Alice in Wonderland*). The main character travels to a place where nothing makes sense, eventually learning how this new world works and returning home the richer for it.

o Comedy (*The Blues Brothers*). A humorous character triumphs over adverse circumstances, resulting in a happy conclusion.

o Tragedy (*Hamlet*). A character with a fatal flaw is undermined by their own mistakes.

o Re-birth (*A Christmas Carol*). The hero goes through a personal transformation that makes them easier to relate to and which saves them from tragedy.

You can see how by using one of these seven key plots you'll find it easier to tell a story around your archetype and product than if you were to start from scratch. They've been proven to work over hundreds of years, so it makes sense to use them.

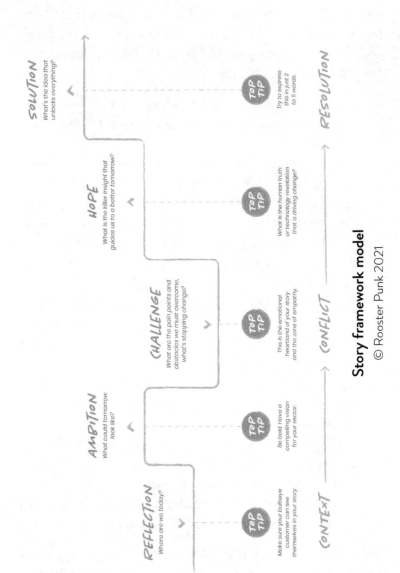

REFLECTION
Where are we today?

Make sure your bullseye customer can see themselves in your story.

AMBITION
What could tomorrow look like?

Be bold. Have a compelling vision for your sector.

CHALLENGE
What are the pain points and obstacles we must overcome, what's stopping change?

This is the emotional heartland of your story and the zone of empathy.

HOPE
What is the killer insight that guides us to a better tomorrow?

What is the human truth or technology revelation that is driving change?

SOLUTION
What's the idea that unlocks everything?

Try to express this in just 3 to 5 words.

CONTEXT → CONFLICT → RESOLUTION

Story framework model
© Rooster Punk 2021

The five-stage story tool

Now it's time to think about how you're going to tell your story, which is where our five-stage story tool comes in. This format isn't something we've created from scratch (the source is unknown), but we have adapted it to B2B needs. It's a story arc that reflects, for instance, how Steve Jobs used to present his Apple product launches, and the line represents the emotional journey he took people on.

o Reflection: where are we today? Letting your customer know where you're at and that you're talking to *them* is vitally important at the beginning of your story. For instance: *CMOs all over the world are struggling to use brand as a growth enabler in their businesses.* If you were one of those CMOs you'd know this is relevant to you, because it's talking about a problem you can identify with. Notice how the CMO is positioned as the central character of the story from the beginning.

o Ambition: what could tomorrow look like? Next, give your audience a sense of ambition. *Imagine if the world of B2B marketing led with brand not product; imagine if every company had a strong sense of purpose; and imagine if every business connected emotionally with its customers and had amazing stories to tell.* You should be bold and paint a compelling vision for your sector.

o Challenge: what are the pain points and obstacles we must overcome? What's stopping change? This takes your audience from a high to a low, increasing the story's emotional charge; it's the key zone of empathy. It also emphasizes the scale of the problem your company is solving. *But do you know what? This is the reality today. B2B companies sell products based on speeds and feeds, and focus only on their performance marketing levers. How are we ever going to cut through this short-termism and introduce long-term brand thinking to companies? It seems like there's no way forward.* Your audience will be nodding here.

o Hope: what is the killer insight that guides us to a better tomorrow? This raises the emotion again by creating a sense of hope. It's the moment at which you present the insights, truth or killer piece of technology that changes the game. *But there's a new truth in B2B marketing. It's that people don't just want to buy from you, they want to buy into you. They're looking to connect with brands on an emotional level, not just a transactional one.* Maybe all is not lost after all.

o Solution: what's the idea that unlocks everything? This is your unveiling – the solution that your brand holds to your audience's problem. In Jobs' case it was the new iPhone, but in our case it would run like this: *Brand is a company's future cashflow – it should be unique to the business and not able to be copied. It helps companies to connect emotionally with their audiences, turning them from functional businesses into meaningful ones. This significantly increases their growth potential.*

When we write stories for clients we always try to do it in five slides. We start by looking at their marketing materials and sales decks, and see that they usually begin with their product or solution. But starting there means their audience can't see themselves in the story – there's no emotion or ambition, and no storytelling techniques to release the right neurotransmitters at the right times. Instead, we start with their customers.

The framework also allows you to adapt the varying focal points of the five stages to suit your needs. When we tell a brand's story, the way we do it depends on how far the company is on its journey. If it's in a new marketplace and there are no case studies because few people have used their product, the story would be based on ambition and imagining what the world would be like with the new solution. In a mature market, however, we'd create the same level of ambition but talk more about the problems people face when they don't have the product.

In addition, whenever we approach a new client brief we always start with the *feeling* its customer wants to have by the end of the story, never with the product. That way, the brand will own this feeling. Suppose the client's audience is made up of CEOs of large organizations. Our job is to work out the state of mind these CEOs are currently in and work out what positive feeling we need to put in its place. Maybe they're frustrated and the emotion we want them to have is one of joy; this gives us a way into the content. We can then retrofit the product to the storyline, with the product now taking on more meaning because of its association with a positive feeling.[9]

The 13 stories

Our experience of creating stories for brands has also led us to think about all the different kinds of B2B stories there are to tell. We've come up with 13 main groupings, although we recognize there are many sub-stories within each heading.

o   Origin: providing the foundation for all your brand activity.

---

[9] You can use Robert Plutchik's famous 'wheel of emotions' to help you decide which feeling to move your audience from and towards: https://buffer.com/resources/science-of-emotion-in-marketing

o   Purpose: creating an emotional message that goes beyond profit.

o   Contrast: bringing life to your point of difference.

o   Product: communicating the nuts-and-bolts of your service.

o   Empathy: relating to your customers by humanizing your offer.

o   Innovation: projecting your journey to greater growth.

o   Focus: achieving a balance between specialist expertise and wider appeal.

o   Culture: empowering employees to become passionate ambassadors.

o   Compassion: sharing your social impacts to give customers confidence.

o   Planet: highlighting the role your brand plays in sustainability.

o   Impact: championing successes future customers can identify with.

o   Reach: clearly communicating your routes to market to build trust.

o   Authority: using thought-leadership to edge out the competition.

The point of this list is that it illustrates that you have far more than your product story alone to tell. If people start buying into you as an organization, not just as a seller of products, they're also buying into a whole host of stories about you. You don't need to concern yourself with each and every one of them, but it's helpful to see the wide range of narratives that you have at your disposal to humanize your brand. For instance, if you're a high-tech business with a strong R&D heritage, your innovation story would be of most interest as it sets you apart. However, your focus story would also be relevant, especially if you operate in a niche market; it could explain why you're in that sector and what you're doing to improve people's lives there. Plus there will be many more stories you can develop to showcase all aspects of your brand.

Some effective storytelling

Storytelling is one of those things that's best learned through an example, so here we'll walk you through a case study which shows how we've made storytelling work for an inspiring brand.

Incopro is a software tool that enables businesses to prevent online fraud and brand infringement, allowing them to protect their digital channels and IP, and to guard against fake websites and imposter products. Described like that it sounds pretty dry, and Incopro didn't want it to be. They approached us to help them humanize their brand so they could attract a new swath of customers who would normally never consider a solution like this.

We saw that Incopro needed a new strategic positioning and a re-brand, which started with clarifying the reason for its existence as a company. It soon became apparent that the product wasn't just a software solution but a calling to unite other businesses in the fight against bad actors in the industry. Together we developed their purpose, mission and vision.

o Purpose: to make the Internet better for businesses and their consumers.
o Mission: to help global brands come together and win against the people and organizations who abuse

their brands, copy their products and put consumers at risk.

o Vision: to create a world in which consumers can trust every online interaction with a brand, and in which businesses can invest in their brands without fear of copycats or infringers stealing their consumers and damaging the trust they've worked so hard to win.

This evolved into a story revolving around a 'join a bigger gang' ethos, and we created a storybook to help Incopro's executives and employees understand and articulate the new positioning. It starts by setting the scene and describing how the business, since its inception, has been working to make the Internet a better place. Drawing parallels with the Wild West, it also emphasizes the new risks for online brands from online criminals, thieves and scammers who are trying to rip them off. The problem has now reached a scale at which it's too overwhelming for brands to deal with on their own, which is where Incopro comes in. Incopro's approach is different: by forming a united front with other businesses and by using its software platform, all companies can join together to put pressure on the criminals and eventually defeat them.

This is a strong story in its own right, but to bring it fully to life we created a new website and marketing assets to help Incopro deliver the message. Crucially, the website is fronted by a video which summarizes the story for potential customers who are interested in knowing what the business can do for them. It's immediately clear that Incopro isn't just another platform provider offering a list of technical features and benefits (although it does have those, of course), but a brand with meaning and purpose. If you were a business owner who's worried about what would happen to your company if it fell victim to scammers or copyright infringers, you'd feel a strong sense of relief and belonging when you saw what Incopro had to say about itself. You can see this for yourself at www.incoproip.com.

The ten new rules of storytelling

Let's start to bring what we've learned to a head. Storytelling has plenty of so-called rules: archetypes, story arcs, narrative types – the list can seem endless. However, we've developed an overarching set of rules – the ten new rules of storytelling – especially for B2B marketing. Actually, they're not really rules but inspirational north stars to guide you on your journey to becoming an accomplished storyteller.

1 Go story

The best brands propel themselves forward by creating and telling stories, not just by talking about features and benefits. Once you have a level-one (organizing) story to tell, you can bring it to life with a stunning identity, tone of voice and memorable experiences.

2 Walk the hard path

You can't simply rely on a good product to dominate your category. Great companies dig deep, and poke and prod, until they uncover their true purpose, a sense of mission and a clear vision of how the world will be better with their business in it.

3 People rock

The best brands are people-made and people-powered. Their employees and customers are their go-to storytellers. They're the frontline ambassadors on which everything hinges. If you can make them feel part of something meaningful and give them the freedom to live your story, your business will know no bounds.

4 Emotion is where the game is won

People buy with emotion and justify with fact. If you want to engage with people, you have to find a way to shift the conversation from the technical to the emotional. It's like the wings of a bird: you need both types of content if you want your business to fly.

5 Reality check

Forget what you're trying to sell – nobody is really that interested.

6 Be a story maker

There's a saying that 'The brand is what the brand does'. Your challenge is to improve the lives of the people your business touches, so that they have stories to tell as well.

7 Everything starts with the customer

First, last and everything. If you're the most important person in the conversation, it's time to leave before you're booted out.

8 Show up happy and positive

As the challenges of life become ever more complex, people find comfort in brands that show a positive and upbeat view of the world. In fact, research shows that 49% of people are willing to pay more for a brand with positive values.[10]

9 People can smell your bullshit a mile off

Be truthful and sincere, or risk being alienated from your market.

10 People buy stories just as much as they buy products

Let your customers see themselves in the story you're telling.

You've probably recognized quite a few of these rules from what you've read so far, so there should be nothing surprising here. But it can be empowering to see these ideas in one place, because – if nothing else – they show how the principles of humanized marketing and great storytelling are one and the same.

Story hunting

Many organizations find it difficult to know where to find authentic stories, and this is where story hunting comes in. It's based on the fact that you already have plenty of

---

[10] Hebblethwaite, C. (2017). '49% of Consumers Willing to Pay More for a Brand with Positive Values', MarketingTech, 22 May. https://marketingtechnews.net/news/2017/may/22/49-consumers-willing-pay-more-brand-positive-values/

stories available to you, both internally and externally, and you just need to find them.

If you're a large organization, there will be hundreds of amazing stories sitting in your teams that have never been told before. Some of your employees have done extraordinary things, from raising money for charity to overcoming serious personal challenges. These can reflect positively on your brand, because the logic is that if these people work for your company it says a lot about the kind of business you are. These stories aren't always easy to find, but when you unearth them they're like hidden gold, and it's your job to mine that seam. We've found that the process of doing this helps employees connect with one another by creating conversations, so it can be a valuable exercise in its own right.

If my memory serves us rightly, several years ago, SAP (the software giant) ran a campaign in which it created stories around 50 of its employees who were doing amazing things. Then it dedicated the front page of its website to them. Visitors arriving at the site were presented not with the usual corporate waffle about ERP Software, but with insights and stories about the interesting people who made up SAP. Remembering that 70% of the B2B buying journey has already taken place before a prospect makes contact with anyone in sales, you can see how this human, story-based view of the business would have made a significant impression on prospects' brand choice. SAP gave itself an advantage by connecting on a human level.

It's the same with customer stories. Talk to them and find out what they think about you. Large companies such as Oracle and Microsoft have customer reference programmes which are responsible for creating case studies, testimonials and references, and these can be used by sales people or put onto their websites. In B2B, peer-based recommendations are invaluable, as are the opinions of influencers in the market. Being able to identify those influencers and be part of their success story, so that they recommend you to others, is the ultimate advantage. Every company should be a story maker if it can.

The power of creativity

The strategy for your brand storytelling is your starting point, but after that there's the telling. What makes your story unique isn't just your raw materials, but the way you assemble and apply creativity to them. It would be perfectly possible to tell a dry, boring story even if it had wonderful ingredients, but that would be a waste. Your stories should be compelling content because not all stories are equal, just as not all products are equal.

You have to make your story stand out so it's the most interesting in your sector, and it's creativity that allows you to do that. For instance, surprise is a brilliant way of catching people's attention. If you'd visited the SAP website expecting to see a bunch of boring statistics, you'd have been taken off-guard by the interesting and creative stories there instead. You might have told your colleagues and given some of them a read.

We've given you various examples of how stories can live in different formats, such as video, web pages, thought-leadership content, events, customer interactions and presentations. However, in the future, storytelling will become more immersive through the use of different technologies. Maybe you'll walk into a travel agent and be given a set of virtual-reality goggles, which will take you to the places you're thinking of going. You'll be living your future story in 'real life'.

This is just one of the many reasons why we're so excited about telling stories that have never been told before. In fact, it's a real honour to be a part of the process.

Key takeaways

o Stories are the ultimate humanized branding device because they make your facts memorable, they give your audience reasons to care, they cut through to people's inner psyches and they build your brand.
o Stories can be grouped into three levels: organizing, in-market and tactical.
o There are many models and tools for structuring a story, such as archetypes, plot outlines and the five-stage story tool.
o There are at least 13 different types of story you can tell in your business.
o The ten rules of storytelling sum up everything that's fundamental in stories and brand building.
o You can discover countless stories within your employee and customer base.
o Creativity is how you make your story sing.

The likeability factor

Have you ever seen the film *The Imitation Game*, starring Benedict Cumberbatch? It's the one about British mathematician Alan Turing, who cracked the German Enigma code and saved countless lives during World War II. In it there's a pivotal moment when he's at the pub with his soon-to-be-bride Joan, who can see that he's onto something huge, even though he's struggling to get it off the ground. At this point she says to him, 'It doesn't matter how smart you are. Enigma is always smarter.' Her message was that he couldn't crack the code on his own and therefore needed to win over his colleagues to help him, but the problem was that he wasn't a likeable kind of person so they weren't on his side. Later, of course, he galvanized them into action, but to me this is the essence of what likeability in brands is about. Your product can be the cleverest, most technical and most advanced in the world (just like Alan Turing), but if people don't like you as a business they'll take their custom elsewhere. As we've said before, people don't want to buy *from* you, they want to buy *into* you.

The idea that we would give our business to companies we like, even if they don't necessarily offer the best performance, might seem strange, so let's take a look at likeability from the perspective of people rather than brands. It's pretty obvious that we naturally gravitate towards the ones we like and away from those we dislike (and if someone falls into neither camp, we're neutral). What might seem less obvious is that likeability actually trumps all other factors. In his book *Likeonomics*,[1] Rohit Bhargava references a 2005 study in which employees from four large organizations were surveyed. Based on how they answered questions and on how their peers rated them, the participants were ranked by two characteristics: competency and likeability. Then they were asked to imagine that they had a job to do at work. Which of their colleagues would they choose to team up with? Unsurprisingly, everyone chose the highly likeable and highly competent people ('Lovable Stars'), and no one wanted the low-competence and low-likeability ones ('Incompetent Jerks'). However, what was unexpected was that, when faced with a choice between working with someone who was likeable and someone who was good at their job, the employees uniformly chose to work with the low-competence and high-likeability people ('Lovable Fools'), rather than their opposites ('Competent Jerks'). In other words, they opted for likeability over skill, talent and experience.

We do this all the time. In politics we vote for the most likeable politicians, as evidenced by the landslide victories of Tony Blair and Boris Johnson. We often shop in stores, or eat in restaurants, where we warm to the staff because they give us great service even if the prices are higher.

[1] Bhargava, R. (2012). *Likeonomics: The Unexpected Truth behind Earning Trust, Influencing Behaviour, and Inspiring Action.* John Wiley & Sons, p. xxxiii.

When we buy in a business context it's no different, apart from the fact that the individual people behind the product aren't always visible to us. This means that the brand has to do the likeability job.

Your customers make their buying decisions based on which company or brand they like the best – it's as simple as that. To a certain extent this has always been the case, but it's become especially important today. Over the past ten years there's been a massive shift in the way that buyers think, act and feel about business brands. A new type of millennial decision maker is in the ascendant and they want you to be different; this can already be seen in the gradual move away from macho, 'alpha' brands like Oracle and IBM, and towards 'beta' B2B brands like Salesforce which are more in touch with their customers' emotions. In complex and digitized markets such as technology and financial services, likeability is especially critical. For many years companies relied on expensive sales people to create the likeability factor, but today, when communications are usually online rather than face-to-face, they recognize that they need to invest in their brands to deliver a positive and friendly experience.

This means that it's a fundamental requirement for your brand to be liked, not for the sake of it but because it gives you a commercial advantage. In this new era it's important that you think of business not as a sales game to be won or lost, but as a popularity contest in which you always need to be evolving, to have a voice and to be relevant.

We recently met the CEO of one of the new wave of empathetic fintech companies. The company has a long-established competitor so you might imagine they would find it hard to gain a foothold, but they found the opposite to be true. 'Everywhere we go, people like us because we're offering something fresh and different in a stale world. We win business not because we're better than the incumbent, but because people instantly like us more than them. We're different and interesting.'

In this age of equivalence, when most companies make strikingly similar products and services and sell them at homogeneous price points, how do you imagine people make the decision to buy from you? The truth is that they come to you if they like you. What's more, brand likeability is about more than just attracting customers; it also gives a structure to how you embrace techniques such as storytelling and measurement to drive your future growth.

What likeability is not

When we talk to people about the importance of likeable brands, we find there are often misunderstandings about what the word means. We'll explore what makes a brand likeable in a moment, but let's look first at what being likeable is not.

For a start, it doesn't mean being smarmy, manipulatively charming or nice to people with the expectation of receiving something in return. We've all experienced this kind of approach from people we know, and it's just as off-putting from brands. You have to be believable and authentic; you can't fake your way into people's hearts. Nor is the aim of likeability to make your company superficially popular by racking up approval on social media. The old world was about social vanity, but the new one is being liked for what you stand for, what you do and how you show up. You should be thinking 'likeability', not 'likes'.

Interestingly, there's another aspect to likeability that you might not have thought of, which is that you don't necessarily need to be nice to be likeable. Steve Jobs was a notoriously difficult person to work with, but was greatly liked by his employees because he always told the unvarnished truth. He had the best intentions of his business at heart, and never expected anything more from other people than he was willing to give himself. In the Netflix series *The Last Dance*, basketball star Michael Jordan created the same kind of likeability. People admire those who are ultra-committed because they inspire trust, admiration and respect; maybe you know someone like that yourself.

This, however, is not *carte blanche* to create an amazing product that has no likeable element to it. For a start, it's extremely rare to be as likeable as Jobs while also being a pain. And we'll never know for sure, but Jobs might have found it easier to influence people if he'd been a pleasant guy *as well as* being a brilliant innovator. Bringing this into the sphere of brands, you can see that even if a product is far superior to its competitors in every way, it has to work extra-hard if it's not likeable; this puts a huge amount of pressure on it to outperform others in its sector. And for what? Why make your brand into a 'Competent Jerk' when you could increase your sales and protect your market position by being a 'Lovable Star' instead?

The B2B likeability gap

The challenge for the vast majority of B2B companies is that they've never made any significant effort to be liked; instead, they've had a blind obsession with their products at the expense of everything else. This has had a disastrous effect on customer trust across all sectors, because marketing's done such a bad job over the years that most people don't believe anything that companies say. This is why platforms such as TripAdvisor and GlassDoor exist: customers believe what their peers say about businesses more than they trust the businesses themselves. There's a massive likeability gap, or rather a truth gap, between what companies say they do and what they're actually like.

This isn't what customers want. The link between strong branding and likeability is shown by the 2020 Edelman Trust Barometer's special report on brand trust during the COVID-19 pandemic.[2] During this time, 81% of people said that they must be able to trust a brand to do what's right, 71% said that brands and companies that place profits before people will lose their trust forever and 89% wanted to be informed about how brands are supporting and protecting their employees and customers. In other words, the message to brands is to 'show up and do your part; don't act alone; solve, don't sell; and communicate with emotion, compassion and facts'. People have always wanted to trust and like the brands they have dealings with, and the current situation amplifies this. The message to take away from this is that people are crying out for you to be likeable. In B2B, even

[2] Edelman (2018). '2019 B2B Thought Leadership Impact Survey', 5 December. www.edelman.com/research/2019-b2b-thought-leadership-impact-study

more so than in B2C, we crave comfort and certainty in what we buy – we need to trust our suppliers because our careers depend on it.

Despite this dismal scenario, the last few years have seen some consumer brands making a concerted effort to be more likeable. As consumers themselves, your customers have experienced this and appreciated it. But when they turn up to work they don't get that same vibe from B2B brands, and they wonder why B2B can't do what B2C is managing to achieve. The gap is alarming. They want to be entertained, surprised, educated and rewarded in the same way as they are when they visit their favourite retailers or brand websites, and can't understand why they're not. Instead, they're faced with a wall of B2B marketing that's been obsessed with the speed of scientific and technological progress for so long that it's forgotten about the timeless qualities of empathy and compassion. This is in fact good news for you, because it means you're pushing at an open door if you can make your brand more warm, friendly and inviting.

The clock is ticking for B2B. The most likeable brands will be the ones that win, which means that if there's nothing much to like about your business you'll eventually be ousted by one that shows some humanity. In the words of entrepreneur Peter Shankman, you need to 'Stop chasing likes and start doing more likeable things.'

What it means to be likeable

Some years ago, Saatchi & Saatchi created the notion of Lovemarks, or brands that inspire 'loyalty beyond reason'. Lovemarks are the brands that deliver way beyond their customers' expectations, and reach out to people's hearts by creating an intimate, emotional connection that 'you just can't live without'. They're the entities that, if they were to disappear, would leave a hole in people's lives.[3]

Being honest, it's hard to imagine anyone loving a B2B brand in quite this way, but we can certainly aspire to create likeable ones. So what are the factors that influence likeability from a brand perspective?

What the experts say

The concept of likeability is a relatively new one for experts to explore, and we're learning more about it ourselves each day. We've been inspired by those who have written in depth on the subject, so we'll start by referencing them here.

Likeonomics author Rohit Bhargava has created five principles for what makes a likeable person or brand, and which together make up the acronym TRUST.

o Truth. This inspires trust, but Bhargava makes the point that being truthful goes deeper than sharing honest facts. Truth is more fundamental and emotional than that. Sometimes the most human thing a company can do is to admit an 'inconvenient truth' about itself, and commit to putting it right. This can create an enormous amount of likeability and long-term loyalty.

o Relevance. To inspire liking in others you have to know what they're thinking and feeling right now, because

---

[3] Saatchi & Saatchi (n.d.). 'Lovemarks'. http://saatchi.co.uk/en-gb/purpose/lovemarks

without an understanding of the context they're operating within, you can't deliver the messages that are relevant to them. This means listening first so that you build understanding, and only then putting across your point of view in a way that matters to them.

o Unselfishness. People now expect companies to behave in an ethical and altruistic way. They can tell the difference between compassionate and helpful acts which are designed for effect, and those which are given with a true spirit of generosity.

o Simplicity. Stripping away complexity makes your product easier to use and relate to, and therefore easier to like. People appreciate the effort it takes to make things simple because it shows you care.

o Timing. This combines convenience and relevance. When you say or do something likeable at the right time and in the right way, it amplifies the effect. A good example is when a business carries out a charitable activity that's especially relevant to its time, such as a clothing manufacturer making protective equipment for hospital staff during the COVID-19 pandemic.

Bhargava also references interesting research done by others on what makes brands likeable. In the 1990s, three researchers in the Netherlands carried out studies for the Advertising Research Foundation. Their results, published in 2006, proposed that there were four components to likeability in advertising: entertainment, relevance, clearness and pleasantness. Our interpretation of this in a B2B context is that entertainment is not only about surprise and fun, but also education; relevance is about speaking to prospects in a way that enhances their experience of your brand right now; clearness is about simplicity and ease of communication; pleasantness is about being a warm and friendly brand to deal with.

As you can see from this, there are various opinions on what makes a business likeable, a point borne out by a piece of academic research called 'The Brand Likeability Effect: Can Firms Make Themselves More Likeable?'[4] In this, the authors attempt to create the parameters for what likeability consists of. They conclude that we evaluate the likeability of brands in two main ways: through source stimuli and through psychological evaluation. When we experience a brand we find it likeable if we appreciate its credibility, attractiveness, similarity (with what we think), familiarity, expertise, trustworthiness and fairness. This all makes sense, but they also go on to make the point that it's other people who also influence our evaluation of a company. If these people are trusted by us and are seen as having an educated point of view, it will increase the likeability of a brand as well.

The seven likeability factors you can't do without

Reading and thinking about the concept of likeability, including how we've brought it to life in the brands we've worked with, has led us to create the seven factors you need to consider if you're to create a brand that people are drawn towards. You won't necessarily need all of them, but you should think in terms of having at least three or four.

[4] Nguyen, B., Melewar, T.C. and Chen, J. (2013). 'The Brand Likeability Effect: Can Firms Make Themselves More Likeable?', *Journal of General Management*, 38(3): 25–50.

1 Helpfulness

When someone helps you, you're forever grateful to them, and brands are no different. If you can be someone's knight in shining armour in their hour of need, or even just a supporter on a general basis, they'll feel warmth and loyalty towards your company for a long time to come. You can be helpful in various different ways: by going the extra mile, doing favours and paying it forward through your ethical business activity. This also helps to trigger the reciprocity effect.

2 Being there

Feeling truly listened to is a rare experience, so showing that you know your audience so well that you can show up at the right time, and in the right way, is impressive. It's like you've read their minds, saving them the trouble of explaining themselves.

Bear in mind, though, that being there for people means walking the talk. Writing about how you want to help people without doing much about it is simply 'helpwash'. Your customers' needs are specific and time sensitive, so if you can't address them in a relevant way it would be better not to try.[5]

3 Generosity

---

[5] Harrison, J. (2020). 'Authentic, Helpful, Humble and Human – the Keys to Great B2B Messaging in the Era of Coronavirus', B2B Marketing, 11 May. www.b2bmarketing.net/en-gb/resources/blog/authentic-helpful-humble-and-human-keys-great-b2b-messaging-era-coronavirus

When companies do things for us without expecting anything in return, we feel like returning the favour in the form of our custom and attention, and even our recommendations to others. Businesses can do this through their corporate social responsibility and social activities. By default, all commercial entities are seen as grasping and selfish, so any brand that acts in an overtly genuine and generous way has an instant advantage.

4 Over-commitment

In his brilliant book *Eating the Big Fish*, Adam Morgan (1999) makes the point that all businesses can commit to something, but it's the ones that over-commit that win our attention and admiration. In our view, over-commitment is such a powerful word. When you're doing something don't just commit to it, over-commit to it: go all in and put your heart and soul into it. People love companies that are so enthusiastic about what they do that they seem to eat, sleep and dream it. Challenger and cause-based businesses have a real advantage here.

5 Honesty

Likeability and trust are two sides of the same coin, and honesty is the hand that flips it. It's so rare to think that a business is telling the truth, that if you can cut through the cynicism and convince people you're being completely honest, you'll create a tribe of advocates. These are the customers who will buy from you again and again, recommend you to their colleagues and even forgive you for your mistakes.

6 Humanity

There's so much that you can do to make your brand likeable just by the way you talk to people, whether it be through your sales team, on your website or with your other marketing communications. Using warm, everyday language, avoiding jargon and making sure your focus is on your customer rather than just on your product all go a long way.

7 Teaching your stuff

We can't help but like and admire people who are experts in what they do, and we follow their lead. This is why we pay attention to testimonials and credentials when we're deciding who to buy from. However, what we find truly likeable is when people turn themselves from being 'just' experts into being teachers, by packaging up their knowledge in a relevant and entertaining way and sharing it with us. This should be the essence of thought-leadership.

The four types of likeability

The seven likeability factors are useful when you're working out how you're going to turn your brand from cold and clinical to warm and human, but where should you place your focus? It depends on where your company is currently at, what kind of brand you have and what else is going on in your sector. Look around you – what would make you likeable within your category? Each brand should have its own flavour of likeability; you should be taking the core idea of your brand and story and making it likeable in your own way.

This is where it's helpful to consider what we call the four types of likeability. Which is the one that would most suit your brand and product?

Instant likeability

You know how some people are instantly likeable? You only have to meet them for the first time, and before you know it you're telling them everything about yourself and introducing them to your friends. These people have the X-factor with likeability, and they've most probably developed it unconsciously – it's an integral part of their personality.

Some companies have this too – they're intensely likeable in an instinctive way. Maybe they simply use a choice word here and there on their website, or a piece of imagery that strikes a chord with their audience. Sometimes the effect is all the more charming because not much thought seems to have gone into it. But as these businesses grow they need to find a way of scaling their likeability by becoming more deliberate about it, much like a startup has to consciously manufacture a culture as it expands. They have to manage their likeability in all aspects of their companies: their brand image, their product design, their people and their content – without losing the magic along the way.

Likeability factors to focus on: helpfulness, generosity, honesty and humanity.

Earned likeability

This is when your brand becomes likeable over time through the effort you put into it. Your company could have a dogmatic adherence to the truth no matter how unpopular it may be. You could show an over-commitment to a cause, or challenge the status quo, revealing a passion for what you believe in above all else, like The Body Shop did. Or you could demonstrate an amazing level of helpfulness to people, leading them to feel reciprocity towards your brand. This is especially effective if it's both personalized (in other words, directly relevant to your audience) and unexpected (we all love pleasant surprises). A good example is from car-hire company Avis: 'We Try Harder'.

Likeability factors to focus on: helpfulness, being there, over-commitment and knowing your stuff.

Compassionate likeability

When you have a reputation as a compassionate brand, it means that people see you as a company that puts its own interests second and the wider good first. You view the world through a larger prism than pure profit, gearing your efforts towards making a positive difference through the enactment of your overarching purpose. This is a likeable position to be in because it generates trust; a company that goes out of its way to help others is one that can also be relied upon to treat its customers well. It has a warm and caring glow around it.

Another way to look at this is to imagine you bump into the CEO of a company that you want to do business with and have a minute to impress them. Do you reel off your usual elevator pitch, full of buzzwords and 'benefits'? Or do you offer them something of value instead? Something that would be meaningful to them as a person, such as the opportunity for one of their teenage children to do an internship in your business? If it's the latter, you've hit on a home truth. It's emotionally intelligent to apply your brand in a way that creates a valued exchange – this is what creates compassionate likeability.

Likeability factors to focus on: helpfulness, being there, generosity and humanity.

Challenger likeability

This is when you achieve likeability by virtue of the fact that you're the non-conventional player in your industry. Instead of going with the crowd, you've identified an unconscious need – something your audience didn't even know it wanted until it saw it – and jumped into a space that's badly served by others. You're challenging the norm. There's an inherent likeability involved with being a challenger because people love an underdog, and they can see you're committed to serving your customers above all else. By doing the right thing rather than following the crowd, and by being a trusted educator who tells your customers what they really need to know, you become a likeable brand.

Likeability factors to focus on: over-commitment, honesty, humanity and knowing your stuff.

You'll have noticed that each of these types of likeability inspires trust in its own way. Brands with instant likeability prove they understand you, those with earned likeability win you over through reciprocity, those with compassionate likeability show you they care about you and those with earned likeability gain your respect.

You can also create different kinds of likeability throughout your marketing activity. Your website should create 'instant', your brand should create 'earned' (because you always deliver against your purpose and values), your customer service teams should create 'compassionate' and your sales teams 'challenger'. Your job is to pull these elements together so that your business becomes unstoppable.

The measurement of likeability

Given how fundamental likeability is to a brand's success, it stands to reason that you'd want to measure it. A likeability index or framework would give you and your team something to measure your efforts by, and become a focus for your activity just like your net promoter score and other KPIs are for your marketing.

Before we get too wrapped up in the idea of measurement, though, let's take a reality check on the notion of putting a yardstick to the concept of likeability. In *Likeonomics*, Rohit Bhargava tells an interesting story about the genesis of the term 'return on investment' (ROI). Apparently it was created in the 1970s by a man called Jack J. Phillips as a way of describing the business value of intangible activities that didn't lead directly to product sales or the winning of new customers. In other words, it was designed for the opposite of what it's come to mean since then, which is a way of measuring hard business results for pretty much everything.

The problem with using ROI in a blanket way, regardless of context, is that it isn't always relevant. There are some things that we invest in because we know it's the right thing to do, even if they're intangible and non-measurable. Or, as Gary Vaynerchuk is reported to have said: 'What's the ROI of your mother?' Surely it's obvious that not all activities can be ROI-ed, but that doesn't mean we shouldn't value them.[6] It's like a company balance sheet that includes revenue and expenditure figures, but not how engaged the company workforce is. And yet the leadership still focuses on engagement because it knows it will bring more profits and is the right thing to do.

Another aspect of measurement that troubles us is that it can lead us to apply metrics without considering the downsides, as Bhargava explains. For instance, if you're wanting to lose weight, you know that reducing your calorie intake would be a good idea. Taking this to the extreme, you might decide to consume nothing all day but diet sodas – this would surely cut your calories right down. It would, but at what eventual cost? You'd be better off eating healthy food and losing weight without becoming malnourished. Another example is the obsession that many marketers have with dwell time on their websites. The standard thinking is that the longer people spend on your site, the more engaged they are, but is that true? Some visitors might have found it hard to discover what they needed, spending 20 minutes clicking around in frustration before leaving forever. Others might have spent 30 seconds finding exactly what they wanted and left delighted. The figures don't tell it all.

[6] Bhargava, R. (2012). *Likeonomics: The Unexpected Truth behind Earning Trust, Influencing Behaviour, and Inspiring Action.* John Wiley & Sons, pp. 50–51.

A framework for likeability

Having said all this, we still think it would be a good idea to have some way of measuring likeability so that businesses have a checklist of factors they need to develop in order to humanize their products. This is pretty easy for existing customers; the net promoter score is in effect a measure of likeability. In the world of prospects, however – which, as we've seen, is the main B2B audience brands should be focusing on – there's no such way of evaluating how likeable people find a company.

This is why we need a likeability index, so that all businesses can see which activities are leading to their brands becoming favourably viewed by people who haven't bought from them yet. It would be a universal measure of brand strength and equity, and a simple and effective way of communicating the power of a B2B brand. After all, the more likeable a company is, the more opportunities it has to win new business.

Key takeaways

o Likeability is what draws people to your product, far more so than whether you outperform the competition on speeds and feeds.
o Likeability is not being smarmy or charming for the sake of it.
o Likeability involves helpfulness, being there, generosity, over-commitment, honesty, humanity and knowing your stuff.
o You can have instant, earned, compassionate or challenger likeability.

o   Measuring likeability is a good aim, as long as you analyse the results in the context of what you want to achieve with your marketing activity.

The undeniable facts

We hope we've convinced you that humanizing your marketing is something you have to do if you want to make a dent in the universe. However, we realize it's not just you we have to win over. We've been in the B2B game long enough to know that there's a host of other decision makers sitting behind you who also need to be persuaded to make this mindset shift, and who haven't had the benefit of reading this book. One answer, of course, is to pass it to your CEO or CFO. Another is to present the business case to them in the language they understand the best: data.

There's credible, research-based evidence from influential names such as the B2Bi @ LinkedIn and Google proving that all B2B companies have the potential to transform their sales if they take a more emotional and empathetic approach to their marketing. You'll have noticed that we've brought the results of these studies into various parts of the book already, but it can also be helpful to have them collected in one place. This is your go-to reference chapter for all things fact- and data-related when it comes to humanizing B2B; we suggest you use it to shore up your next marketing presentation to the board.

The two main pieces of B2B research are the Binet and Field study carried out for the B2Bi @ LinkedIn, and

Google's 'From Promotion to Emotion' report. We'll explore these here, together with some interesting statistics from other research studies, and conclude with some pithy observations about what they mean for you and your CEO.

'The 5 Principles of Growth in B2B Marketing'

This study[1] is the 'steak in the sandwich' of B2B marketing research, in that it's the most recent and also the most on-point in terms of validity, detail and the areas it covers. Carried out in 2019 by the B2B Institute on behalf of LinkedIn, and led by marketing luminaries Les Binet and Peter Field, it sets out to answer two main questions.

o 'If we all instinctively agree that strong brands influence what companies we buy from, partner with, invest in, or decide to work for, why isn't there more evidence-based research on this topic?'
o 'Why does B2B marketing, an industry that is worth billions, seem to lack a coherent understanding of how brands create growth over time?'

To do the research, Binet and Field used the UK IPA Databank, one of the world's best sources of information on marketing effectiveness. It's made up of data submitted over 40 years as part of companies' entrance into the IPA Effectiveness Awards, and contains the results of almost 1,500 marketing and advertising campaigns. Although the

---

[1] Binet, L. and Field, P. (2019). 'The 5 Principles of Growth in B2B Marketing: Empirical Observations on B2B Effectiveness', The B2B Institute and LinkedIn. https://business.linkedin.com/marketing-solutions/b2b-institute/marketing-as-growth

number of B2B campaigns in the Databank is relatively small, it still shows some interesting patterns, especially in comparison with successful B2C campaigns.

We'll go into the detail in a moment, but if you're interested in the upshot, it's this: most B2B marketers are doing the exact opposite of what's recommended in the research report. Binet and Field point out that brand building is a long-term strategy that pays off in years, but that only 4% of B2B marketers measure impact beyond six months. They also highlight the importance of new customer acquisition strategies, and the relative ineffectiveness of loyalty ones. And yet only 52% of B2B marketers believe that reach is a strong predictor of advertising success, and over 65% think that businesses grow by increasing loyalty, not through attracting new customers. If you're one of those marketers who's brave enough to reject the group-think that's evolved in B2B over the last couple of decades, you have a career-making opportunity ahead of you if you use this research to guide you.

The report starts by asking the question: 'why advertise?' In B2C, advertising has long been seen as one of the most effective tools for growth, but in the world of business it's been assumed that rational business buyers aren't influenced by emotive ads. At first, the study says, companies can succeed without brand advertising because sales tend to be generated through word of mouth and repeat business. But eventually a brand reaches the point at which innovation slows, costs have been driven as low as they can go and the low-hanging customer fruit has been picked. This is when advertising becomes essential, and the purpose of Binet and Field's research was to establish what a B2B business should do at this point. This resulted in its five principles of growth in B2B, which we covered in the chapter 'The new truth' and will expand upon here, together with some helpful visuals.

1 Invest in share of voice

In B2C, brands that set their share of voice (SOV) above their share of market (SOM) tend to grow, and those that set their SOV below their SOM tend to shrink.

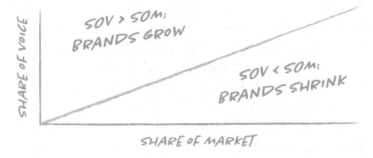

Share of voice versus share of market

Source: Binet, L. and Field, P. (2019). 'The 5 Principles of Growth in B2B Marketing: Empirical Observations on B2B Effectiveness', The B2B Institute and LinkedIn. https://business.linkedin.com/marketing-solutions/b2b-institute/marketing-as-growth

However, is it the same in B2B? The answer is yes, with a strong correlation shown between market share growth and 'extra' share of voice (ESOV) for B2B brands. The conclusion you can draw from this is that when you're setting your advertising budgets, you need to take into account the market share you want to attain and then estimate what you need to spend in order to achieve it. That's how you'll generate the growth you're after. One of the most interesting areas of development that complements this thinking is called share of search as a predictor of market growth.

2 Balance brand and activation activity

Sales activation is any activity that's aimed at achieving an immediate purchase response, and its ROI can be high. However, the effects are short-lived because the campaigns aren't memorable and they therefore don't do much for a brand's long-term growth. In contrast, brand building activity is designed for long-term growth, working on an emotional level to influence people's thinking about a product or company long after the campaign has ended. Although it's more demanding and requires greater investment than activation, it's ultimately more effective because it builds over time. It also reduces price sensitivity, leading to the potential to earn higher profits. In essence, think of your brand as your future cashflow.

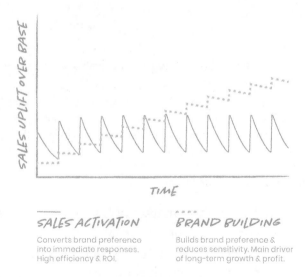

Marketing works in two ways

Source: Binet, L. and Field, P. (2019). 'The 5 Principles of Growth in B2B Marketing: Empirical Observations on B2B Effectiveness', The B2B Institute and LinkedIn. https://business.linkedin.com/marketing-solutions/b2b-institute/marketing-as-growth

You need both types of marketing to succeed both short- and long-term, and because brand building is more costly it should receive more budget. In B2C this is usually 60%, but Binet and Field's research suggests that – as an approximate, guiding principle – B2B efficiency is maximized when around 46% of the budget is allocated to brand and 54% to activation. We're willing to bet that 46% far outstrips what you currently invest in brand building.

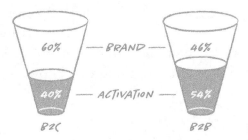

In B2B, the investment balance skews towards activation, since sales is harder.

Brand building versus activation

Source: Binet, L. and Field, P. (2019). 'The 5 Principles of Growth in B2B Marketing: Empirical Observations on B2B Effectiveness', The B2B Institute and LinkedIn. https://business.linkedin.com/ marketing-solutions/b2b-institute/marketing-as-growth

3 Expand your customer base

The accepted wisdom in marketing as a whole seems to be that it's more profitable to grow by selling more to existing customers than it is to expand your customer base itself. Binet and Field point out that extensive research by the Ehrenberg-Bass Institute shows that, for B2C brands, the opposite is true. Growth is mainly achieved by acquiring new customers and – along the way – gaining a bit more business from existing ones. But is this also the case for B2B? The data says it is.

To come to this conclusion, the researchers used a measure of effectiveness called the 'Number of Very Large Business Effects', which tracks significant movements across six indicators from sales to profits. This shows that, in B2B, customer acquisition campaigns are much more effective than loyalty campaigns. In fact, the latter had a success rate of zero on this measure.

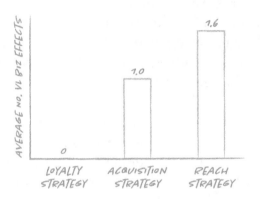

Targeting new versus existing customers

Source: Binet, L. and Field, P. (2019). 'The 5 Principles of Growth in B2B Marketing: Empirical Observations on B2B Effectiveness', The B2B Institute and LinkedIn. https://business.linkedin.com/marketing-solutions/b2b-institute/marketing-as-growth

The Ehrenberg-Bass research goes further, in that it also shows that the way to grow is to appeal to as many category buyers as possible, rather than trying to own a segment of the market. This means that you should talk to as many people as you can, knowing that the majority of your audience will be new prospects but that your advertising will also reassure existing customers that they've bought into the right brand. You may wonder if this means you should be investing in mass-market advertising for your B2B brand, but Binet and Field advise caution here. Your category buyers might be a small niche, and your choice of media should reflect that. However, remember that the average decision making group in large enterprises is now ten people, so marketing to one bullseye customer doesn't make sense.

4 Maximize mental availability

Mental availability is a measure of what impact your campaign has had on those who've seen it. As we've explored, human beings don't use logic to make decisions; they use mental shortcuts instead. One of the outcomes of this is that, given a choice between several options, people tend to go for the one that comes to mind most easily. We know how important this is in B2C marketing but what about B2B, where decisions are more fully considered and researched? The research shows that even though B2B buyers are somewhat more rational than B2C, campaigns that increase a brand's share of mind are the most effective; the more famous they make the company, the better the business results.

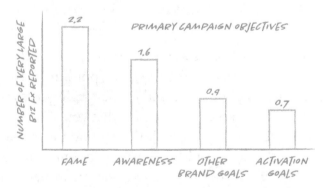

The relationship between brand mental availability and growth

Source: Binet, L. and Field, P. (2019). 'The 5 Principles of Growth in B2B Marketing: Empirical Observations on B2B Effectiveness', The B2B Institute and LinkedIn. https://business.linkedin.com/marketing-solutions/b2b-institute/marketing-as-growth

5 Harness the power of emotion

In our view, this principle underpins the whole research piece. Binet and Field point out that the aim of advertising is to create preference for your brand, and that the most effective way of doing this is to build associations between your product and the feelings that encourage people to buy it. They also assert that although it's been assumed for a long time that decision making in B2B is far more rational than in B2C, the IPA Databank suggests this is only slightly the case. What matters here isn't functional messaging, but emotional.

It's worth breaking this down into short-term sales activation and long-term brand building. In the former, rational approaches such as product and price messages can work well, but this isn't the case for the latter (and vice versa). The authors refer to Daniel Kahneman's model which shows that if people like a brand, they hold positive beliefs about its benefits; therefore, advertising that encourages warm feelings towards your brand will also encourage them to think your products are worth buying. Then, when you release a sales activation campaign, they'll respond to it positively because they're predisposed to think well of your product. The two types of campaign help one another to work harder.

Binet and Field give examples of effective emotional angles that have been used in successful B2B brand building campaigns.

We have the human touch in a tech-obsessed world

We understand that it's a tough world in business

We empathize with the loneliness of a business leader

We know the challenges of entrepreneurship, so we champion entrepreneurs

This emphasis on emotion can be a difficult one to swallow for many B2B marketers. However, we're not saying that rational messaging has no role to play, but that it should be limited to short-term activation. Before your product is launched, start priming prospects with emotional advertising, then when they come to buy, serve them with persuasive product messages that help to make the sale. The 46% brand and 54% activation ratio we referred to earlier shows that rational messages are slightly more important in B2B, but also that emotional messages are far more influential than they're given credit for.

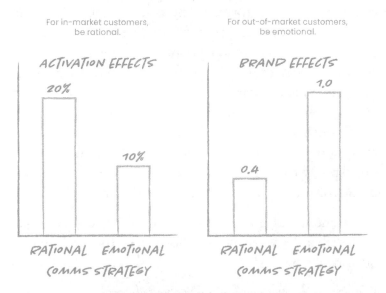

For in-market customers, be rational.

For out-of-market customers, be emotional.

ACTIVATION EFFECTS

20%

10%

RATIONAL EMOTIONAL
COMMS STRATEGY

BRAND EFFECTS

1.0

0.4

RATIONAL EMOTIONAL
COMMS STRATEGY

Rational versus emotional messaging

Source: Binet, L. and Field, P. (2019). 'The 5 Principles of Growth in B2B Marketing: Empirical Observations on B2B Effectiveness', The B2B Institute and LinkedIn. https://business.linkedin.com/marketing-solutions/b2b-institute/marketing-as-growth

Interestingly, inspired by Binet and Field's research, UK-based marketing agency The Marketing Practice has also carried out a study into B2B effectiveness.[2] This compares the attitudes of B2B marketers who outperform their competition with those who don't. The agency found that the outperformers were long-term thinkers who were twice as likely to see campaign measurement as lasting longer than six months, and were also twice as likely to dedicate more than 60% of their budget to achieving long-term goals. Given the longer sales cycles in B2B versus B2C, this makes sense to us.

At this point we'd like to give our thanks to the B2B Institute in conjunction with LinkedIn, as it's doing a brilliant job of creating noteworthy industry content that's pushing our thinking about B2B marketing in a new direction. We'd also like to mention that the work of author and creative thinker Orlando Wood is highly relevant if you're interested in learning more about creative effectiveness.

'From Promotion to Emotion: Connecting B2B Customers to Brands'

This is another highly revealing piece of research, carried out by Google in 2013 along with CEB's Marketing

---

[2] The Marketing Practice and *Marketing Week* (n.d.). 'The Long and Short of B2B Marketing'. https://themarketingpractice.com/insights/the-long-and-the-short-of-b2b-marketing

Leadership Council and research firm Motista.[3] It set out to discover whether B2B marketers are correct in assuming that focusing on business value is the best way to differentiate their brands, or whether emotion should be playing a bigger role in their marketing. To do so, Motista surveyed 3,000 purchasers of 36 B2B brands across multiple industries, and compared the results with its existing B2C databank.

It discovered that, much to everyone's surprise, B2B brands actually drive *more* emotional connections than B2C. Most B2C brands have emotional bonds with between 10 and 40% of consumers, but some of the B2B brands have over 50%. This is because when a consumer makes a purchase the stakes are relatively low, but when a B2B customer puts their reputation on the line by spending a lot of money on a product, they won't do so unless they feel a substantial element of trust to balance out the risk.

The study also highlighted that while it's often assumed that B2B purchase decisions are mainly driven by maximizing business value, business buyers don't perceive much functional difference between the products they could buy to fulfil their requirements. And yet this is where most B2B marketing activity is focused. Instead, B2B marketers need to build emotional connections by ramping up the anticipation of the rewards to be gained by buying their products, through emphasizing the feelings associated with them. The crucial point here is that B2B

---

[3] Nathan, S. and Schmidt, K. (2016). *'From Promotion to Emotion: Connecting* B2B *Customers to Brands'*. CEB Marketing in Partnership with Google and Motista. www.thinkwithgoogle.com/intl/en-gb/consumer-insights/consumer-trends/promotion-emotion-b2b/

buyers are almost 50% more likely to buy a product or service when they're convinced of its personal value to them, such as the opportunity to advance their careers or boost their reputation – so much so that they're eight times more willing to pay a premium for it.

When you realize that by leading with emotion in your marketing you're delivering what B2B buyers already want (and practise), you should have more confidence to go down this route. In effect, you're pushing at an open door.

'The "State of B2B" Survey 2019 – Winning With Emotion: How to Become Your Customers' First Choice'

Specialist market research agency B2B International, in conjunction with B2B creative agency Gyro, surveyed 2,000 decision makers across a variety of functions, sizes of business and countries. Together they wanted to discover what factors influenced the decisions of B2B buyers and how important emotion was in driving their behaviour.[4] Their key finding was that 56% of the final purchase decision is based on emotional factors. They also learned that different factors drive decisions according to what stage of the purchase journey the B2B buyer is on, as follows.

First, your brand has to be visible and memorable even to be considered; 95% of decision makers say they have to feel an emotional connection to a supplier's brand before

---

[4] B2B International (2019). 'The "State of B2B" Survey 2019 – Winning With Emotion: How to Become Your Customers' First Choice'. www.b2binternational.com/the-state-of-b2b-survey-2019/

they first contact them, and that this is as important as feeling confidence in the company's ability to deliver.

Second, the supplier that establishes a thought-leadership position is the one most favoured when creating a shortlist. This shows that price isn't the most important factor, but rather the value the buyer thinks the brand will add to their business. Notice that it's the things that matter most to your audience, and that you can also deliver, that will best differentiate you from the competition.

And finally, by the point at which you're one of the few companies that's asked to provide a formal proposal, you've already passed the basic tests and there's probably little to separate you from your main competitor. This is where emotion comes in again. Although you still need to satisfy your prospects' needs for experience, specification and service, you also need to build a strong emotional connection with them. This accounts for 56% of the final decision.

So what are these emotions that are so influential in the final purchasing choice? The researchers identified them to be trust, confidence, optimism and pride: trust in your credibility as an organization, confidence in your ability to deliver, optimism about what you can do for them and pride in the prospect of working with you. If you're able to stimulate these four emotions in a prospect, you'll increase your chances of winning their business by 50%.

Aggregated research

In addition to the primary research we've covered above, there's an insightful piece of secondary research by B2B agency Earnest, a company that produces an annual roundup of data and statistics gleaned from various sources.[5]

Earnest's starting point is that trust in B2B brands is at an all-time low: 58% of buyers and decision makers don't trust their claims, even if they already work with them. Instead, buyers put their faith in themselves when they decide who to do business with. The vast majority do their initial research online, and want to stay anonymous during this part of the process; 94% say they dislike giving out their details in order to download content, and 25% lie about who they are when they do so. What's more, most don't trust ads, and half say the content they receive is useless, even though it would have had a significant impact on their buying decision if it hadn't been. Given this, what can you do to be the brand they trust? There are five factors to focus on.

o Deliver a great experience by making buying easy. You're 62% more likely to win the sale if you do, and your customers will spend 140% more with you.

o Be the most helpful; 97% of B2B buyers want content that contains solutions and tips, and also makes it easy for them to convince others internally to buy from you.

o Content is good as long as it's the right kind; 46% of buyers prefer short content and 59% would rather watch a video than read a blog post.

o Selling is still important. Even if most buyers don't really like sales people, 76% find it helpful to speak to one, especially if they offer them insights about their industry.

---

[5] Earnest (n.d.). "'Playing hard to get'": Vital Statistics for B2B Marketers: 3'. https://earnest-agency.com/campaigns/vital-statistics

o Consider all decision makers in the sale. While 64% of senior executives have the final say on B2B purchases, 81% of the people who inform their decision internally aren't senior. In fact, 77% of them are millennials.

The report rounds off with a set of insights that you'll be familiar with by now. B2B buyers are 50% more likely to buy when they see personal value in a purchase; a little emotion goes a long way; always remember that business people are people who just happen to be at work.

What this means for you

The facts speak for themselves, but what do the studies mean for B2B in practice? Here are our top takeaways from these pieces of research.

Emotion is excellent for business

It's through tapping into your prospects' feelings that you encourage them to notice you, like you, explore you and buy from you. What's more, they'll pay a higher price for your product than if they don't feel an emotional connection. Rational messaging plays a part but it's only half the story. Neglect emotion at your peril.

It's about long-term breadth, not short-term depth

Reaching as wide an audience as possible is far more successful in the long run than focusing on existing customers through short-term tactical campaigns. You should be thinking about your brand in terms of years, not weeks or months.

Familiarity is the new fame

B2B buyers are just like anyone else – lazy thinkers. Given a choice between considering a business they've never heard of and buying from one they already know and like, they'll do the latter. Your job is to make your brand familiar.

Storytelling is the key that unlocks the treasure chest

Emotion-based marketing can never live without stories, because storytelling is the language of emotion. Build your brand around a series of narratives that resonate with your audience's feelings and encourage them to feel warm towards it, and you've created the bedrock of a successful business.

Being human is profitable

Imagine you're a B2B buyer who has a choice between two brands. If you already like one of them and have an affinity with it, you're more likely to pay attention to its claims and view it positively. You'll also pay a premium for it. This doesn't make you unprofessional, it just makes you human. All B2B businesses should be human in order to sell to other humans – it just makes sense.

In summary, there's so much data that supports taking a more human view of B2B marketing that we wonder why more people aren't doing it. If you, or your CFO and CEO, are wedded to the rational approach, maybe this research will change your mind.

Rise up B2B

This much we know: if B2B marketing is to dodge the meteor that's heading in its direction, it must be about people, not just products. But what does a human B2B product and brand look like? What characteristics does it have? How would you recognize one if you spotted it in the wild? Here's how we see it.

It's very, very good at what it does

It astounds you with its ease of use, delights you with its charm and personality and excites you with the way it maximizes your potential at work. It's dedicated to making your work and life happier, sweeter and more productive.

It's honest and straightforward

It doesn't blind you with science or impress you with complex features or meaningless numbers. Rather, it tells you about itself – what it's like, how it's made and what difference it wants to make in the world. It doesn't pretend that it's anything it's not, but nor does it hide its light under a bushel. If it's brilliant, it will tell you why.

It's appealing

It comes across as warm and friendly, the sort of brand you'd like to have a chat with or ask advice from. It doesn't try too hard, but wins your respect as a result of its likeability. It's forever showing up at the right place at the right time, and it speaks to you in the everyday language you understand. It loves to tell stories that enchant and engage you.

It over-commits

It puts its heart and soul not only into helping you but also into educating you, enabling you to learn so that you feel good about yourself. It throws itself into its purpose, bringing you the very best of what it has in that moment. It's forever looking to improve, to offer you more and to be the only one you recommend to your colleagues (or the one you hide from your competitors). And it will never stop doing it, recognizing that delivering long-term value far outweighs the benefit of making a quick buck today.

It connects

It understands what you really want, even if you don't know it yourself. It realizes that you need ease and simplicity, the ability to achieve more than just the basics of your job and to feel part of something bigger than yourself. Because it's a good listener, it's quick to learn what works for you and what doesn't. It knows itself, and it knows you.

As you can imagine, this lesser-spotted B2B brand isn't commonly seen, but we're sure you wish there were more versions of it around. Its nature fulfils everything we've described in this book, most of which, by the way, isn't new – it's simply truth after truth after truth, packaged up in such a way that it makes sense. If this thinking were mainstream, marketing would be the engine of growth in B2B across the world and marketers would be the people who were most excited of everyone about going into work, because they had such innovative and worthwhile jobs.

And yet, haven't we heard some of this before? So why has nothing changed? For the past ten years we've seen a few brave agencies, brands and marketing leaders fight the good fight to take B2B marketing somewhere new, but their efforts have never managed to turn humanized B2B into the established norm. It will take a concerted effort and high ambitions to effect a mass breakaway from the current model. Now is not the time for us to hide under the shadow of the inferiority complex we've developed after years of comparing ourselves to our more exciting B2C counterparts, and even to our own internal sales teams. We need to take up the challenge.

This is more important now than it's ever been. Consultancy Deloitte's report '2021 Global Marketing Trends'[1] outlines for CMOs the new themes arising in marketing across the world. It emphasizes that, in an age overwhelmed with data, the human experience is critical to brand success, and identifies seven key trends to help companies 'refocus on the human'. Two of these trends underpin all the others: having a core purpose that directs

---

[1] Deloitte (2021). '2021 Global Marketing Trends'. www2.deloitte. com/us/en/insights/topics/marketing-and-sales-operations/ global-marketing-trends.html

every choice a business makes, and a human experience which weaves that purpose across a brand's relationships with all the people it touches and serves. It makes clear the fact that the more human a business is, the more money it will make.

We think it's time that everyone in B2B did something about the current state of affairs, and we hope you agree. We want you to join us in our quest to humanize B2B – to rise up against the endless features and product-centric messaging. And we'd love it if you would join us in shining a light on B2B talent, on customers and on your own learning and leadership potential. When we rise and shine as a collective we can build great B2B brands, so let's take B2B somewhere new and unlock transformational, not incremental, growth.

We want to build a group of activists, evangelists, innovators and rebels across all areas of B2B marketing who believe in the cause of humanizing it – not because it's the latest fad, but because it's the only sustainable direction of travel for our industry and will create the step-change growth every business brand deserves. By donning the mantle of a humanized B2B marketer, you're fulfilling B2B's potential by creating brands and stories that have meaning – that move people and make them feel as if they're part of something special. After all, we're all human beings with similar needs and desires, few of which are met by reading a two-page data sheet.

You'll not be alone. We're here to provide resources for you in the form of:

o   the latest articles and research that will enable the evolution of B2B into something more human o a collective view of the strategic, branding, campaign and sales enablement work that you're creating to help validate this human approach

o the latest thinking from thought leaders in the B2B sector who are pushing the human agenda – both on the client and agency side

o the most helpful tools, techniques, hacks and how-to guides to inform and educate you, so you can make better decisions and do better marketing

o the thoughts and opinions of B2B buyers and decision makers who are on the receiving end of the marketing that you're creating

Visit www.HumanizingB2B.com for more insights.

Call us optimists, but we've been in love with B2B for years, despite its image problem. It's such an exciting industry, with so much potential to grow and change, that if you're an ambitious marketer wanting to make a big impression and realize your vision, you couldn't be in a better place. This is the future you can create for yourself. So crack on and take B2B somewhere new. It's literally in your hands.

About the authors

Paul Cash and James Trezona are co-founders of B2B marketing agency Rooster Punk. They specialize in helping business and marketing leaders to create transformational growth, by unlocking the power of storytelling and creativity within their organizations. They do this in the most complex of B2B markets, across technology, finance and everything in between.

They call what they do 'Humanizing B2B' and its impact is transformational.

Paul has led a 25-year career in business marketing and entrepreneurship, starting in 1996, when he set up a screensaver software company. After that he co-founded a technology marketing company (Tidalwave), which became the fastest-growing marketing agency in the UK. In 2013, having exited Tidalwave, he set up Rooster Punk with the intention of creating the world's most admired B2B storytelling agency. He's a ferocious optimist, loves solving problems through creativity and jumps out of bed at 6:00 AM every morning. He is an FA qualified goalkeeper coach and runs a youth football team in Surrey at the weekends.

James has a similar pedigree in marketing, having started his career at Saatchi & Saatchi (and leaving when he discovered his boss thought the 'internet fad' was going to go away). Seeing technology as a key solution to the issue of the world's problems, especially climate change, he dedicated the next few years to technology marketing and eventually ran well-respected agency Mason Zimbler, growing it to almost 200 people across several countries. He now runs Rooster Punk with Paul. He's a passionate environmentalist, a worrier about the future (in a good way) and is a community rugby fanatic.

If you'd like to get in touch with Paul and James about brand, marketing or storytelling projects, speaking at events or helping to run training workshops, email us at:

Paul.cash@roosterpunk.com

James.trezona@roosterpunk.com

Or pay us a visit at www.roosterpunk.com

Acknowledgements

Thanks, first and foremost, to some knowledgeable contributors who helped us to sense-check our thinking while we were writing this book. We would like to express special thanks to Ginny Carter for her words and guidance, Yasmine Khan and Mel Trezona for their love, support and calming influence and the whole team at Rooster Punk for believing in our mission. Other key supporters that deserve a special mention include Andrea Allen, Victoria Pattinson, Orlando Wood, Dave Stevens and James Farmer. And finally, the combined wisdom and experience of these B2B marketers, who we interviewed along the way, is not to be underestimated. They are:

o Darryl Bowman, CMO at Receipt Bank
o Jan Gladziejewski, VP Regional Marketing and Communications at DXC Technology
o Joanne Gilhooley, Global Marketing Leader at Microsoft
o Joel Harrison, co-founder and editor of *B2B Marketing Magazine*
o Luke Lang, co-founder and CMO at Crowdcube
o Mark Bogaerts, Director of Brand and Sponsorship at Tata Consulting Services

o   Martin Pitcock, Head of Commercial Excellence, Ecommerce at nets
o   Nick Ashmore, VP of Marketing at ResponseTap
o   Richard Robinson, General Manager at LeadFamly
o   Sally Croft, VP of Marketing, Communications, Government Relations and CSR at Ericsson
o   Scott Allen, Global Marketing Development and Strategy Director at Microsoft

Printed in the USA
CPSIA information can be obtained
at www.ICGtesting.com
JSHW011417160824
R13664500003B/R136645PG68134JSX00031B/5